PUSH

DESTINY IMAGE BOOKS BY DR. N. CINDY TRIMM

The 40 Day Soul Fast

40 Days to Discovering the Real You

The 40 Day Soul Fast Leader's Guide Set

The 40 Day Soul Fast Participant's Guide

Reclaim Your Soul

40 Days to Reclaiming Your Soul

PUSH

PERSEVERE UNTIL SUCCESS HAPPENS

through prayer

CINDY TRIMM

DESTINY IMAGE® PUBLISHERS, INC.

P.O. Box 310, Shippensburg, PA 17257-0310

"Promoting Inspired Lives."

This book and all other Destiny Image, Revival Press, MercyPlace, Fresh Bread, Destiny Image Fiction, and Treasure House books are available at Christian bookstores and distributors worldwide.

Cover concept by Prodigy Pixel.

For more information on foreign distributors, call 717-532-3040.

Reach us on the Internet: www.destinyimage.com.

ISBN 13 TP: 978-0-7684-0429-6

ISBN 13 Ebook: 978-0-7684-0430-2

For Worldwide Distribution, Printed in the U.S.A.

7 8 9 / 23 22 21 20

By the God of your father who will help you, and by the Almighty who will bless you with blessings of heaven above, blessings of the deep that lies beneath, blessings of the breasts and of the womb. —GENESIS 49:25

*Honoring the capacity of the human spirit
and the potential hidden within.*

CONTENTS

FOREWORD

Perseverance, endurance, persistence, and faithfulness—these are the common denominators of every individual who receives answers from God and who successfully completes his or her God-given assignment. Most of the requirements of those characteristics aren't visible to the casual observer—although the results certainly are. This is because those who surmount obstacles and opposing forces, which cause most people to give up, do so through prayer. These are individuals who navigate spiritual terrain from a divine perspective. Refusing to become a victim of circumstance, they have acquired the skill of discerning the opportunities that present themselves in the midst of the greatest challenges.

Too many aspiring ministers neglect even the simple, natural process of prayer. There are many vital aspects to successful ministry, but prayer is absolutely essential. God Himself speaks to us through His Word that He will hear and answer prayer. His promise is clear— He will reward those who diligently seek Him (Hebrews 11:6). The

Almighty sent His Son as our professor of prayer in the university of spiritual warfare and successful living (Matthew 6:9-13). Prayer is His guarantee of victory to everyone who will pray without ceasing (1 Thessalonians 5:17). And He will receive all who come to Him with a contrite heart filled with faith.

I often ask myself, "Why won't people pray?" I have yet to find a satisfactory answer to that question. Pray and watch heaven move! Heaven is pregnant; the earth groans and travails as the world awaits the next innovators, spiritual and moral leaders, educators, scientists, and all those who will provide divine blueprints for our global destiny. Pray and feel hell quake. Pray and invite the supernatural to invade the natural realm. Pray and see every circumstance arrayed against you by the advancing armies of the alien antichrist be transformed by the very omnipotence of our eternally self-existent God.

Too many today simply do not wish to exercise the spiritual grit of perseverance and the muscle of prayer to do what is essential to receive and walk in the power of the anointing and the presence of the Holy Spirit. Dr. N. Cindy Trimm is one who understands the centrality of passionate prayer to be an effective minister of the Gospel of Jesus Christ, and to carry the mantle of His glory. This, and much more, you will find demonstrated throughout the following pages.

Dr. Trimm has an authentic writing style that any reader will relate to and enjoy. She explains scriptural principles in ways that any university professor of the Old or New Testament could appreciate. And she offers practical advice for moving beyond the bounds of "ordinary" to achieve the vibrancy and vitality of life lived anticipating the extraordinary.

If you are pregnant with purpose, creative vision, and innovative ideas given to you by God, I congratulate you for choosing Dr. Trimm to be your "literary midwife" (to borrow her term) and guide you through the process of the breakthrough you have believed for—whether that breakthrough is spiritual, relational, or financial. I believe God our Father—the Abba of Jesus—is about to accomplish something supernatural in and through you as you allow Dr. Trimm to guide you into the heights of the manifested tangibility of God through prevailing prayer—as you *persevere until success happens.*

DR. ROD PARSLEY
Pastor, World Harvest Church
Columbus, Ohio

INTRODUCTION

That's why I don't think there's any comparison between the present hard times and the coming good times. The created world itself can hardly wait for what's coming next...meanwhile the joyful anticipation deepens. All around us we observe a pregnant creation. The difficult times of pain throughout the world are simply birth pangs. But it is not only around us, it's within us. —ROMANS 8:18-25 THE MESSAGE

It is amazing to me what great things come forth from the tiniest of packages; things you can't see, or perhaps even imagine, all begin in the obscure darkness of the smallest of containers. There is incredible power and beauty resident in what may seem like a dormant cocoon—nature's womb of beauty and incubator of divine purpose and splendor. Like a grain of seed that is sown in the ground,

13

life begins to stir, silently pushing against the confining barrier, and after what seems a lifetime of waiting, breaks through to grow into something magnificent. Heat, gravitational opposition, and pressure cooperate with God's symphony of life. Energy is ignited. Life is triggered. A mysterious internal mechanism gives forth to a brand new creation—a unique expression of the Master Creator. A new form emerges, pressing and pushing outward—reaching upward—straining toward the light. Energized by the silent force of metamorphosis, a new creation emerges—bursting forth from what seemed dark and confining.

Everything you see began in seed form. You began as a seed—like a butterfly hidden in a cocoon; only you were hidden in a womb. All we are given in this life are seeds—seeds of potential, seeds of ideas, seeds of dreams. The key to a meaningful and joy-filled life is learning to unlock the potential of the seeds of possibility we've been given; to see beyond the exterior surface—or interior walls—of a mundane, nondescript cocoon, into new paradigms of power and majesty. Imagine the butterfly, once a caterpillar—a slow-moving worm—that undergoes such a process. Imagine the paradigm shift of having once been limited to crawling along the ground—then after a season of toil, being stripped of everything familiar, hidden in obscurity, imprisoned in solitary confinement, and then fighting with every ounce of strength to escape...finally emerging with wings to fly! Each of us must undergo the same process in our lives. We are all like the butterfly that must struggle to break through temporary confines in order to spread our wings and take flight. Earth is our metaphorical chrysalis. There will be seasons of toil, letting go of what we hold dear, of obscurity and confinement, and fighting to break free. It is how we become more. It is how we grow our *spiritual* wings. It is how we learn to fly and soar to new heights in God.

Each of us must learn to give birth to our own potential, purpose, and destiny in some of the most challenging circumstances. We must learn to embrace God's wisdom and His provision of grace that helps us to push through barriers. We must learn to yield to the capacity-and-character-building process that ultimately strengthens and enables us to become more than we were before. To give birth to new possibility, new hope, new life. In order to do that, we would do well to learn from midwives who understand the birthing process—who understand the inner workings of the womb and the process of labor and delivery, because like a cocoon, the womb is an incubator of unlimited potential.

It is for this reason I have written *PUSH*—as a field guide for those who want to overcome their struggles, to push past barriers and tap into new realms of possibility; for those willing to learn how to persevere through prayer.

I have taught a great deal on the correlation between intercessory prayer and giving birth. Originally, I titled this book, *The Anatomy of Intercessory Prayer: The 26 Wombs of the Spirit*, because, as you'll read in the chapters ahead, I explore in detail the anatomical process of praying until the solution materializes—or more accurately, *persevering until success happens* through prayer.

As we go deeper into the book, we will discuss what I have designated as twenty-six wombs of the spirit; each I believe will open new doors of revelation to help you embrace the powerful potential residing in each "womb." My intention in writing this book is to provide you with a literary midwife to help you push through your circumstances and bring forth all that God wants to birth in and through you. I hope to help you see with new eyes all that is possible, to build your capacity to conceive, believe, and achieve more, and to give you a new mindset and paradigm for turning problems into possibilities—and to see each as a new opportunity. My desire is to help you see that the pain and darkness you thought were working against you are the very crucibles from which new life emerges.

As I've read about the lives of great achievers, I have learned they all have one thing in common. Each one had to overcome some kind of challenge that threatened to derail them and cause them to abort their purpose. Had they followed the road of least resistance or given in to their emotions, our world would not be as rich and vibrant as it is today. Although we may not recall the names of each individual who has contributed to the progress of humanity, had they not followed the inner promptings of destiny and purpose—that small seed of potential lying dormant within them—we would not have the discoveries, inventions, art, technology, innovations, treatments, cures, or beauty that make up all that is good and life-giving in human civilization as we know it.

I have no doubt that God is the source of all inspiration. After reading so many biographies, it has become clear to me that throughout history, those who have made the greatest impact did so by faith. They had to push beyond the known into the unknown. They had to find hidden reservoirs of strength in order to surmount the seemingly insurmountable. Like so many I've had the privilege to read about, I too have had to dig deep into the reservoir of my faith to muster the energy and courage to face challenges, overcome obstacles, and push beyond my comfort level in order to accomplish a specific goal.

I have lived long enough to know that life is dynamic and not static. Nothing and no one remains the same—we are constantly changing and growing. Growth requires us to build our capacity to become more than what we have been. Even when it feels like we are stagnating, the most challenging thing can be to take that next step forward. We are always challenged to push ahead and press toward that higher calling.

Therefore, in order for you and I to face those challenges, to maximize our potential—fulfill our purpose and realize our dreams—we must remain in peak spiritual, physical, and mental condition so that we can push beyond thresholds of comfort and pain into new places of power in God. If you dare to believe that God has something great in store for you to do, to accomplish, or to achieve, you must be prepared to persevere in spite of your setbacks and challenges. This book is written to give you that extra push—to help you give birth to your dreams and accomplish your goals.

Like Calvin Coolidge, I have learned:

> Nothing in this world can take the place of persistence. Talent will not; nothing is more common than unsuccessful people with talent. Genius will not; unrewarded genius is almost a proverb. Education will not; the world is full of educated derelicts. Persistence and determination alone are omnipotent. The slogan 'press on' has solved and always will solve the problems of the human race.

As Winston Churchill said, "Never, never give up."

Within the pages of this book, you will find biblical examples and biographical sketches of individuals who had to push through adversity, obstacles, rejection, and even bankruptcy in order to realize their dreams. Each one of these individuals has become an inspirational gift to the world, and it is my honor to share their insights with you. Had they not pushed passed their own insecurity, disappointment, frustration, failure—or just the fear of failure—into the promise of their destiny, who knows how dark and empty the world would be today?

If you have picked up this book, could it be possible that on the one hand, like these men and women, you are "pregnant" with a world-changing purpose, a bestselling book, a groundbreaking invention, or an awe-inspiring talent—or perhaps, on the other hand, the earth is pregnant with you? See Romans 8:19-28 Refuse to allow circumstances, challenges, disabilities, rejections, fears, or doubts to abort it.

Just when the caterpillar thought it couldn't possibly become more than it already was, and move past its current circumstances, it pushed beyond the confines of its chrysalis. Drawn upward by the rays of the sun, it leveraged its enormous potential while yet in the throes of a great struggle—it overcame being bound and restricted to emerge a beautiful butterfly. You see, the butterfly was always hidden within the DNA of the worm—but struggle was required to build the strength necessary to be transformed and birthed anew.

No matter what circumstance you find yourself in today, your destiny, purpose, success, and prosperity have been incubated long enough. It's time to PUSH...*Persevere Until Success Happens* through prayer!

The winter solstice has always been special to me...
as a barren darkness that gives birth to a
verdant future beyond imagination,
a time of pain and withdrawal that produces
something joyfully inconceivable,
like a monarch butterfly masterfully extracting
itself from the confines of its cocoon,
bursting forth into unexpected glory. —GARY ZUKAV

The Birthing Process

GIVING BIRTH TO
THE PROMISE

Chapter 1

HEAVEN IS ABOUT TO GIVE BIRTH

There are more things in heaven and earth, Horatio, than are dreamt of in your philosophy. —SHAKESPEARE'S *Hamlet*

Heaven wants to deliver something through you. It is pregnant with the plans and purposes of God. These have grown to full term and are bearing down to be delivered through the Body of Christ. Today, with the world in the state that it's in—with governments crying out everywhere for assistance—I believe the earth is poised to give birth to the kingdom of heaven. For that to happen, however, we must understand the anatomy of intercessory prayer.

We often pray as Jesus told us in Matthew 6:10—*"Your kingdom come. Your will be done on earth as it is in heaven"*—yet we don't fully understand how to give birth to God's will in the earth. Jesus instructed His disciples, *"As you go, preach, saying, 'The kingdom of heaven is at hand'"* (Matthew 10:7). In Matthew 13:31-32, Jesus went on to teach, *"The kingdom of heaven is like a mustard seed…which indeed is the least of all the seeds; but when it is grown it is greater than the herbs and becomes a tree, so that the birds of the air come and nest in its branches."* We carry the seeds of heaven within us; they grow through the study of God's Word and the exercise of our faith, and then the promises and purposes of God are at last manifested through our laboring and travailing in prayer.

Prayer is the process of giving birth to heaven's seed. We understand that when God told Abraham, *"In your seed all the nations of the earth shall be blessed"* (Genesis 26:4), He was speaking of his future descendent Jesus Christ, but that seed lives within each of us who have *"been born again, not of corruptible seed but incorruptible"* (1 Peter 1:23). We are born of and give birth to the promises of God through prayer.

John described the Church in Revelation as a pregnant woman: *"I saw a woman clothed with the sun, with the moon beneath her feet, and a crown of twelve stars on her head. She was pregnant, and she cried out because of her labor pains and the agony of giving birth"* (Revelation 12:1-2 NLT). According to *Matthew Henry's Concise Commentary of the Bible*, this woman represents the Church, "clothed with the sun, justified, sanctified, and shining by union with Christ, the Sun of Righteousness."[1] The Church is called to give birth to the kingdom of heaven in the earth.

Think of Elijah in 1 Kings 18:42, kneeling in a birthing position, *"when he bowed low to the ground and prayed with his face between his knees"* (NLT). Everything that is created is a result of the birthing process. Paul wrote to the Romans:

All around us we observe a pregnant creation. The difficult times of pain throughout the world are simply birth pangs. But it's not only around us; it's within us. The Spirit of God is arousing us within. We're also feeling the birth pangs. These sterile and barren bodies of ours are yearning for full deliverance. That is why waiting does not diminish us, any more than waiting diminishes a pregnant mother. We are enlarged in the waiting. We, of course, don't see what is enlarging us. But the longer we wait, the larger we become, and the more joyful our expectancy (Romans 8:22-25 MSG).

Even as we are being enlarged as a Body, *"the whole creation groans and labors with birth pangs"* (Romans 8:22). More than at any other time in history, we are on the threshold of global transformation. Heaven is indeed pregnant with the fullness of all things. Yet, as God inquired through His prophet Isaiah, *"Shall the earth be made to give birth in one day? Or shall a nation be born at once?"* (Isaiah 66:8). Time is required for a seed to germinate. Solomon wrote that while God *"has planted eternity in the human heart...even so, people cannot see the whole scope of God's work from beginning to end"* (Ecclesiastes 3:11 NLT). Yet God went on to declare through Isaiah, *"Shall I bring to the time of birth, and not cause delivery? ...Shall I who cause delivery shut up the womb?"* (Isaiah 66:9). Although we can't know the exact due date, we can be assured of delivery—but not without the pain of labor and travailing in prayer.

Before Hannah became pregnant with Samuel, she travailed in prayer. From her barrenness, Hannah cried out to God *"in deep anguish, crying bitterly as she prayed to the Lord"* (1 Samuel 1:10 NLT). God was waiting for a woman to pray forth the prophet heaven was ready to give birth to. She consecrated herself, and she consecrated the fruit of her womb, to the Lord. As a result, Hannah became pregnant with a son while heaven was pregnant with a prophet and two kings. Hannah gave birth to Samuel, allowing heaven to birth the prophet who would anoint Saul, and then eventually David, to be kings of Israel. Although she only conceived one child in the natural, heaven conceived triplets in the spirit. If Hannah had not travailed in prayer, she may have never conceived and there may not have been a prophet or a king or a Christ who descended from that king.

The nation of Israel needed a leader, but there had to be a woman through whom God could birth the particular child who would become that leader. This child would become the catalyst that would change the destiny of an entire nation. Not only was this pressing upon heaven, but this was also an urgency in the natural realm, much like what we are experiencing now. The planet is in the throes of a major global crisis—governments everywhere are looking for that man or woman who will provide visionary, moral leadership. This is a global cry. The nation of Israel faced a similar leadership void in its time. Who are these men and women of purpose and destiny whom heaven is wanting to birth? Could it be that while we are waiting for God to intervene, God is waiting for us?

I am convinced that this Scripture is an urgent word for God's people today: *"If My people who are called by My name will humble themselves, and pray and seek My face, and turn from their wicked ways, then I will hear from heaven, and will forgive their sin and heal their land"* (2 Chronicles 7:14). Your prayers move heaven. Similar to the Butterfly Effect, a small action in one part or realm of the universe can produce an exponentially larger impact in another.

Globalization has helped us realize how interconnected we truly are. The Butterfly Effect theory asserts that the fluttering of a butterfly wing in California significantly impacts the weather on the opposite side of the planet—for example, "down under" in Australia. Similarly, the actions and prayers of each one of us can have a profound effect in other hemispheres. We all have a piece of the puzzle. While our piece might not be as astounding as an MIT scientific discovery or as impressive as Gandhi liberating India from British rule, it might be the little things we are birthing on a daily basis that hold the key to healing the social ills plaguing our world today. As the nineteenth-century philosopher William James said, "Act as if everything you do makes a difference. It does."

This raises the question, "What has God put in you?" What are you going through that might be indicative of being in labor in one of these areas? I'm here to tell you that God has seeded you with quantum potential—infinite possibility that need only be captured by the force of imagination, harnessed by the power of faith, and birthed through unwavering belief. Every morning you wake up to unlimited potential and possibilities. From the moment you make a decision, all of those possibilities collapse and bring you an experience or occurrence that is a result of that choice. In *Mother's Intention: How Belief Shapes Birth*, author Kim Wildner writes, "You are constructing your own reality with the choices you make...or don't make. If you really want a healthy pregnancy and joyful birth, and you truly understand that you are the one in control, then you must examine what you have or haven't done so far to create the outcome you want."[2]

Personally, I look at crisis as a divine indication that I need to change something or a divine announcement that heaven is pregnant and getting ready to deliver something to me. All I need to do is adjust the little choices I make every day. Pain does not always equate with something bad; it could simply mean it's time to adjust. It could be an indication that the time has passed for you to be where you are now and that you need to push to the next level. We must be able to clear our minds and hearts of what we feel is the main reason for our struggles or our pain and look beyond to ask whether God is pushing us into a position where we can birth His plans and purposes in the earth.

Is God birthing something through you? Is He trying to show you how you might be the solution to a problem or hold the key to addressing a social ill? Is God trying to get your attention within your family, within your mind, within your church, or some other arena? Are you prepared to receive and then conceive what God is wanting to birth through you?

> *Just as you'll never understand the mystery of life forming in a pregnant woman, so you'll never understand the mystery at work in all that God does. Go to work in the morning and stick to it until evening without watching the clock. You never know from moment to moment how your work will turn out in the end.* —ECCLESIASTES 11:5-6 MSG

> *It is said that the present is pregnant with the future.* —VOLTAIRE

Chapter 2

CONCEPTION: THE SEED WITHIN

You are the gardener of your own being, the seed of your destiny. —THE FINDHORN COMMUNITY

Everything in the universe has been birthed out of the mind of God, *"who kept the sea inside its boundaries as it burst from the womb"* (Job 38:8 NLT). God is a Spirit; therefore, the spirit realm is the causal realm. Everything that was, that is, and that is to come emanates from this spiritual location. All that you see in the natural began as a spiritual seed, a divine thought. In the words of E. B. White, "Before the seed there comes the thought of bloom!" Before the foundations of the world, God conceived a heavenly blueprint for all that exists according to the purpose for which He created it; He contained that blueprint within the seed. Even the kingdom of God starts as a seed: *"The Kingdom of Heaven is like a mustard seed"* (Matthew 13:31 NLT).

It is from the womb of God's mind that the universe was conceived and birthed: *"From whose womb did the ice come forth, and who has given birth to the frost of heaven?"* (Job 38:29 ESV). A womb is a physical *and* spiritual dimension where life is generated, incubated, and developed, awaiting the appointed time and season for manifestation. The words of God spoken forth are like strong spiritual contractions expelling the promise from the womb of conception to the realm of manifestation at the precisely appointed time. It is from this birthing place—what I refer to as the Alpha Zone, for God is the Alpha and Omega—that all things are created and sustained by Him for His purposes. It is also from this place that the power of God is made available to all who would receive it.

The word *conception* comes from the Latin, *concipio*, which means "to receive; to take in; to bring together."[3] To *conceive* is "to receive seed." Paul wrote to the Galatians, saying, *"We receive the promise of the Spirit through faith"* (Galatians 3:14). In other words, we receive Christ, the seed of promise (Galatians 3:16-19), by faith. We consummate our union with God by *taking in* His seed. Paul wrote to the Ephesians, saying, *"[He planned] for the maturity of the times and the climax of the ages to unify all things and head them up and consummate them in Christ, [both] things in heaven and things on the earth"* (Ephesians 9:10 AMP). Our union with God is consummated when Christ is conceived within us.

Christ is the seed of promise from which springs forth the entire will of God for our lives—from the place where "all grace abounds" (2 Corinthians 9:8). Using a symbolic view of obstetrics, I see a room within the Alpha Zone that is like a fertility clinic, abounding with every kind of seed—grace, provision, anointing, and so on. At the appointed time it is from this place that God births into man divine inspiration and empowerment, potential, assignment, gifts, abilities, and purpose. From these seeds, success, prosperity, the ability to subdue and replenish, fruitfulness, multiplication, and dominion are birthed out of man. Look at the seed of genius, the unique intelligence God engineered into every person.

In 1983, Harvard University professor Dr. Howard Gardner published his theory that there are multiple types of geniuses in his seminal work, *Frames of Mind: The Theory of Multiple Intelligences.* Gardner proposed that the traditional notion of intelligence, based on IQ testing, is far too limited. In his original research, Dr. Gardner identified seven core intelligences: linguistic, logical-mathematical, spatial, bodily-kinesthetic, musical, interpersonal, and intrapersonal. Later, however, he added an eighth, the naturalistic intelligence, and suggested there may still be a ninth he termed existential intelligence.

What is your "cognitive profile"? How has God called you to reflect His manifold, or many-sided, wisdom? You are but one reflection of the myriad of faces on the prism of His glory. Become familiar with and operate out of your unique intellectual strength. Get in sync with the wisdom God has ordained for you. Press into God's chambers and pray as the psalmist David did, *"I've been out of step with You for a long time.... What You're after is truth from the inside out. Enter me, then; conceive a new, true life"* (Psalm 51:5-6 MSG).

There is a unique genius that resides within each one of us. This is the seed God has hidden in every individual that the Lord Himself "travails in prayer" over (Romans 8:34), His Spirit coming alongside helping you to push out this new life. It is the unique expression of Himself that He has deposited within you, giving birth to an all-new creation (2 Corinthians 5:17). This mystery is as ancient as it is beautiful.

In the oldest book of the Bible, Job asks, *"Who has put wisdom in the inward parts?"* (Job 38:36 ESV). It is God who puts His Spirit of wisdom within us. In another translation, we read, *"Who gives intuition to the heart and instinct to the mind?"* (NLT). The intuition and instinct at work within each person is distinct to that particular person. As Paul told the Ephesians, *"But to each one of us grace was given according to the measure of Christ's gift"* (Ephesians 4:7). It is up to each of us to discover and cultivate that grace. David wrote, *"In the hidden part You will make me to know wisdom"* (Psalm 51:6). God's grace is germinating in your spirit and soul while it is yet hidden—a mystery: *"Just as you cannot understand the path of the wind or the mystery of a tiny baby growing in its mother's womb, so you cannot understand the activity of God, who does all things"* (Ecclesiastes 11:5 NLT).

God has downloaded all knowledge and wisdom within the depths of our hearts and minds, but we need to upload it and bring it forth into the world. When you conceive a word or promise or purpose from God, you must allow it to mature in your spirit until it has grown to full term and becomes due for delivery. How do you know it's time to be delivered? When you begin to feel pressure, when your life seems to be pressing in as if contracting around you and you feel as if you have entered into a season of hard labor.

God will provide challenges to cause you to tap in to this hidden potential. Editor and author Susan Taylor has famously stated, "Seeds of faith are always within us; sometimes it takes a crisis to nourish and encourage their growth." The seed is the potential that is lying dormant on the inside, the genius sleeping within, the champion hidden within you. Look past the discomfort and awkwardness to see the new life potential you are carrying. Chinese philosopher Lao Tzu recognized that "to see things in the seed, that is genius."

Most people believe the fruit is the most important part of a tree, but the seed is the most valuable because hidden within the seed is the invisible assignment of the tree. In the words of renowned science fiction writer Marion Zimmer Bradley, "Flowers and fruit are only the beginning. In the seed lies the life and the future." A seed not only encapsulates the full-grown fruit, but an entire harvest, a future generation hidden to the human eye. As Robert Schuller once said, "Anyone can count the seeds in an apple, but only God can count the number of apples in a seed."

The power resident within a seed is truly miraculous, yet it pales in comparison to the resurrection power at work within the seed of promise every believer has been impregnated with. It caused Paul to exclaim, *"Glory to God, who is able, through His mighty power at work within us, to accomplish infinitely more than we might ask or think"* (Ephesians 3:20 NLT).

We are told in 2 Peter 1:3-4 that *"His divine power has given to us all things that pertain to life and godliness."* God has already given us everything we need to live a supernatural life in order that we might be *"partakers of the divine nature."* By His nature, God is a creator. He is a creative force awakening to life the germ within every seed and the seed of promise alive in every believer. Be faithful with the seed you are carrying. God could be using the currents, and sometimes torrents, pushing against you to cause you to make some adjustments for the sake of the new life growing within you. Protect and nurture that life force, for it could grow to be a fountain of life in someone else's desert.

Make sure you are conceiving and bringing forth the life of God and not something else. Begin by living and walking in righteousness and truth: *"But You desire honesty from the womb, teaching me wisdom even there"* (Psalm 51:6 NLT). Listen to what the Bible has to say about those who don't walk in the truth: *"They conceive trouble and give birth to evil. Their womb produces deceit"* (Job 15:35 NLT); *"The wicked conceive evil; they are pregnant with trouble and give birth to lies"* (Psalm 7:14 NLT); *"You conceive chaff, you give birth to straw; your breath is a fire that consumes you"* (Isaiah 33:11 ESV); and, *"They rely on empty arguments and speak lies; they conceive trouble and give birth to evil"* (Isaiah 59:4 NIV).

It is God who determines nativity, God who draws us to Him and turns our hearts. He will cause you to hear His voice and walk in His ways if you but open your heart to Him. God will strategically place you in the optimum place to birth His seed and accomplish His will. He carefully provides challenges and problems that will cause you to press down and tap into your greatest potential. At the same time He is always with you, helping you protect and grow the seed He has caused to be sown in your heart. He is a Husbandman and Master Gardner who never fails to make *"everything beautiful in its time"* (Ecclesiastes 3:11).

> *By faith Sarah herself also received strength to conceive seed, and she bore a child when she was past the age, because she judged Him faithful who had promised.* —HEBREWS 11:11

> *If seeds in the black earth can turn into such beautiful roses, what might not the heart of man become in its long journey toward the stars?* —G. K. CHESTERTON

Chapter 3

CARRYING TO FULL TERM

*Life is always a rich and steady time when
you are waiting for something to happen or to
hatch.* —E. B. White, *Charlotte's Web*

*If I had my life to live over, instead of wishing
away nine months of pregnancy, I'd have cherished
every moment and realized that the wonderment
growing inside me was the only chance in life to
assist God in a miracle.* —Irma Bombeck

*All the time we wondered and wondered, who is this
person coming/growing/turning/floating/swimming
deep, deep inside.* —Crescent Dragonwagon

God is raising up the next generation of giant slayers who will champion the cause of the King and His kingdom, those whose agenda is linked to God's overall redemptive plan for His creation.

The Body of Christ is pregnant with the leaders and visionaries who will bring God's purposes to pass in the earth. The Church must be diligent to labor in prayer on behalf of the young captains coming forth from her ranks and mindful not to miscarry or prematurely deliver the future heroes of the faith.

Who are the heroes and giant slayers who will take down the leviathans opposing God's kingdom? David was the youngest and scrawniest of all his brothers and, as a result, was given the lowliest task of wandering the hills with his father's sheep. Yet it was there he learned to kill a lion and a bear. No one paid any attention to him as he sat out there with the sheep. But God was with him, preparing him for greatness. God had planted a seed of greatness deep within him, a seed that sprouted and grew as he fellowshipped with the Lord.

God has planted a seed of greatness within you as well. There is an assignment He prepared for you to accomplish before you were even born: *"Before I formed you in the womb I knew you, before you were born I set you apart"* (Jeremiah 1:5 NIV). You have been endowed with a unique gift that only the Christ revealed through you can deliver. You have been placed on the earth at this time in history, in this generation, *"for such a time as this"* (Esther 4:14). You are not a mistake; you are in the right place at just the right time, having been chosen and called by God *"just as He chose us in Him before the foundation of the world"* (Ephesians 1:4). You are God's champion in whatever arena He has placed you.

Like David, however, there is a season when your potential is hidden, another when it is called out, another of preparation, another when it is tested, and still another season when it is revealed and refined. David was not even considered a candidate when the prophet Samuel came looking to anoint one of Jesse's sons to be the next king of Israel. After Samuel discovered David, there was a season when he lived in King Saul's palace as an armor bearer. It was during this time he proved his valor by slaying Goliath, and when he showed he had greatness beyond that of Saul, he was cast out, chased down, and had to hide out in a cave just to stay alive. It was there David grew close to God and surrounded himself with faithful men who would become the leaders of his mighty army. He became the captain of that group of leaders, and through great trials and battles was at last crowned king. He carried the potential God placed within him to full term.

Just as Paul instructed the Thessalonians, we must not *"become weary or lose heart in doing right [but continue in well-doing without weakening]"* (2 Thessalonians 3:13 AMP). For Solomon wisely stated, *"To everything there is a season, a time for every purpose under heaven"* (Ecclesiastes 3:1). We must learn to be patient, to *"let patience have its perfect work, that you may be perfect and complete, lacking nothing"* (James 1:4).

One of the most difficult mental and emotional challenges during pregnancy is *waiting*. Especially in the last trimester, when the potential is no longer hidden, it is felt on every level—the weight of it is almost unbearable—and still there is nothing to do but wait.

I am reminded of the parable of the sower recorded in Luke 8:5-8, and the myriad of ways the seed of God's Word is lost: it isn't watered, the enemy steals it, and the world's distractions choke it out. It is easy to be deceived by what seem like other priorities or pressing issues. We can be shortsighted, or rather nearsighted, focusing only on short-term concerns rather than long-term goals. James left us with a good piece of advice, however: *"Be patient, brethren.... See how the farmer waits expectantly for the precious harvest from the land. [See how] he keeps up his patient [vigil] over it until it receives the early and late rains"* (James 5:7 AMP). We must learn to be patient and faithfully carry the seeds of promise we are given to full term; we must patiently wait for the fruit to mature before we look for a harvest.

A large part of carrying the Word of God to full term in your life is surrounding yourself with the right kind of support. Too often within your relationship constellation you are exposed to people who have what I call an "abortive spirit"—they have a way of killing your vision, destroying your passion, undermining your sense of direction and identity, or simply dampening your expectations. These individuals might be family members who are verbally or physically abusive, parents who compromised your innocence during childhood, or a spouse or employer who demoralizes you. These are methods the enemy uses to cause you to miscarry the seed of greatness God has planted in your heart—they are abortive in nature.

Some of the world's problems have gone unsolved because individuals who were carrying the assignment to provide the answer were aborted. Leaders, scientists, entrepreneurs, and so on were either aborted or somehow miscarried the assignment. Nations are asking, "Where is the moral leadership in our land today?" Could it be that some of these leaders fell victim to the abortive spirit at work in the earth?

Think about what almost happened to Moses in the Book of Exodus. Pharaoh had all of the Hebrew male infants killed because he feared that a deliverer would rise up from among their ranks. The same thing happened under the rule of King Herod after the birth of Jesus. Sometimes there is a satanic knowledge that a certain generation will birth a leader, and because the enemy doesn't know who in particular that leader will be he will attempt to annihilate the entire generation. We see this happening in our own day throughout the world where the atrocity of genocide is taking place.

This is the abortive spirit that we see at work—not only as a cultural norm that permits individuals to legally abort their babies, but also where entire villages are wiped out. Could it be that there is an expected deliverer who was to be born within that particular village or within that particular generation?

The important thing to remember is that every person has been endowed with a seed of greatness. Each person holds the seeds of an answer, a solution, a message, or a gift—a special assignment involving some kind of delivery. God created each person to be a deliverer on some level in whatever arena or sphere of influence God has positioned him or her. Whatever God has graced you with, value it, nurture it, and bring it to fruition. Paul told Timothy, *"Do not neglect the gift that is in you"* (1 Timothy 4:14). In the words of author and television host Rev. Faisal Malick, "If you are pregnant with a baby, with a ministry, with a task, you have to give birth to it. If you have not felt new life stir within you for a while, allow the presence and the glory of God to revive it, and then pray for wisdom to carry it."[4]

I exhort you to be faithful with the seed God has given you. It contains the assignment He has commissioned you to carry out in this earth. Carry that seed in good soil, water it, protect it, make it a priority, and allow it to grow and mature to full term. Bring to fullness the champion that you are and fulfill the divine mission that only you can accomplish.

> *"Sing, barren woman, who has never had a baby.*
> *Fill the air with song, you who've never experienced*
> *childbirth! You're ending up with far more children*
> *than all those childbearing women." God says so! "Clear*
> *lots of ground for your tents! Make your tents large.*
> *Spread out! Think big!"* —Isaiah 54:1-3 MSG

Pregnant women! They had that preciousness which they imposed wherever they went, compelling attention, constantly reminding you that they carried the future inside, its contours already drawn, but veiled, private, an inner secret. —RUTH MORGAN

Attending births is like growing roses. You have to marvel at the ones that just open up and bloom at the first kiss of the sun but you wouldn't dream of pulling open the petals of the tightly closed buds and forcing them to blossom to your time line. —GLORIA LEMAY

Chapter 4

TRAVAIL

Nearly every revival has been preceded by the physical prayer of travail—an intercessory birthing that not only serves as an outward prophetic sign of what God is doing, but also incorporates the believer's entire body, soul, and spirit in some of the most intense, enjoyable, and beneficial kind of prayer. —JOHN CROWDER[5]

...without darkness
Nothing comes to birth,
As without light
Nothing flowers.
—MAY SARTON

There is a time for conceiving and *receiving seed*, a time for faithfully carrying the seed with expectation, and a time for bringing the seed you are carrying forth, both delivering and being delivered.

Giving birth is a process that does not begin in the birthing room but in the intimacy of a private chamber where an invisible germ of potential is given and received. The birth of new life begins at conception. Godly plans and purposes begin in the prayer closet.

The seed of God's promise for you is planted in your spirit when you receive His Word in the inner sanctum of your heart. It is carried to term through your faith and expectation. And it is delivered through trial and tribulation, or *travail*. We not only travail in prayer but also in life. *Travail* is both defined as "work, especially work that involves hard physical effort over a long period" and "to be in labor" as a woman during childbirth.[6]

We deliver the promise we carry both through travailing experiences as well as travailing prayer. According to Mark 4:17, we undergo *"persecution...for the word's sake."* The enemy strives to stir up persecution against the word of promise about to be birthed through you, the seed you carry in the womb of your spirit containing the life and deliverance God has created you to bring forth. The Rev. Faisal Malick states, "The wisdom hidden within you will bring about persecution and affliction because you are pregnant with something that is not just about you. When you give birth to that word it will bring life to everyone around you."[7]

When you are about to birth your assignment—your prophetic destiny—you will go through a period that can be compared to the dark before the dawn. It is always darkest just before the sun is about to rise. St. John of the Cross called this time "the dark night of the soul." In the words of F. Scott Fitzgerald, "In the real dark night of the soul it is always three o'clock in the morning, day after day." And to quote St. John, "The soul perceives itself to be so unclean and miserable that it seems as if God had set Himself against it."

But we read in Isaiah that God Himself went through this very same thing before the Sun of Righteousness arose in the earth: *"I have long been silent; yes, I have restrained Myself. But now, like a woman in labor, I will cry and groan and pant"* (Isaiah 42:14 NLT). And just before the Son fulfilled His destiny as the Redeemer of humankind, *"He began to be troubled and deeply distressed. Then He said, 'My soul is exceedingly sorrowful, even to death'"* (Mark 14:33-34). Seven hundred years earlier Isaiah had already prophesied, *"He shall see [the fruit] of the travail of His soul and be satisfied"* (Isaiah 53:11 AMP).

We bring forth from our spirit the life God has birthed into our innermost being. When Jesus made the statement, *"From his innermost being shall flow...springs and rivers of living water"* (John 7:38 AMP), what was translated as "innermost being" here is the Greek word *koilia,* which, according to *Vine's Expository Dictionary,* means "womb."[8] Dutch Sheets, in his watershed book *Intercessory Prayer,* writes, "We are not the source of life, but we are carriers of the source of life. We do not generate life, but we release, through prayer, Him who does."[9] Sheets goes on to define spiritual travail as "releasing the creative power or energy of the Holy Spirit into a situation to produce, create, or give birth to something."[10]

Yes, the power of the Holy Spirit is released through prayer, but it is also released when we simply believe and trust in God during a period of difficulty or hardship, such as a time of intense labor. Jesus prefaced the verse where He spoke of living water flowing from our innermost being with, *"He who believes in Me [who cleaves to and trusts in and relies on Me]"* (John 7:38 AMP). We cleave to and trust in and rely on God when we labor in life just as we do when we labor in prayer. By doing so, we release the creative power of the Holy Spirit to give birth to something new through us.

Whatever is born in the natural realm is birthed from the spirit, and by the Spirit, through our travail. It is during these times of travail that we cry out to the Lord and *"groan within ourselves"* (Romans

8:23). Each of us individually is called to labor on behalf of the seed of life we carry. We may suffer in the process, but as the psalmist declared, *"Those who plant with tears will gather fruit with songs of joy. He who goes out crying as he carries his bag of seed will return with songs of joy as he brings much grain with him"* (Psalm 126:5–6 NLV). In other words, there is a season in which we go through pain and hardship carrying the promise God has given us, but in the end, if we continue to trust the Lord of the harvest, we will reap joy and gladness.

Again, Jesus likened our life in Christ to a woman about to give birth:

> *When a woman gives birth, she has a hard time, there's no getting around it. But when the baby is born, there is joy in the birth. This new life in the world wipes out memory of the pain. The sadness you have right now is similar to that pain, but the coming joy is also similar...a joy no one can rob from you* (John 16:21-23 MSG).

Scripture not only speaks about individuals travailing on behalf of the life of Christ being formed within themselves and other believers (Galatians 4:19), but it also speaks of the Church corporately travailing on behalf of the kingdom of God being formed within the earth. When Jeremiah wrote, *"For I have heard a cry as of a woman in travail, the anguish as of one who brings forth her first child—the cry of the Daughter of Zion, who gasps for breath, who spreads her hands, saying, Woe is me now!"* (Jeremiah 4:31 AMP), he was speaking of the Church travailing on behalf of a world pregnant with new souls for the kingdom. Isaiah prophesied the end result of this: *"As soon as Zion was in labor, she gave birth to her children"* (Isaiah 66:8). And as I shared in the first chapter, the whole earth *"groans and labors with birth pangs"* for deliverance *"from the bondage of corruption"* (Romans 8:21–22).

In due time, you and I and the entire earth will be delivered. Through the prophet Isaiah, God made plain the outcome when He offered the following inquiry: *"Shall I bring to the time of birth, and not cause delivery? ...Shall I who cause delivery shut up the womb?"* (Isaiah 66:9). Just as Jesus was *"proof that came at the right time"* when *"He gave himself as a payment to free all people"* (1 Timothy 2:6 NCV), you can be sure that you too will be proven and positioned to deliver at the right time. Of course, that requires you continue to put your hope in God. You must *"labour therefore to enter into that rest"* (Hebrews 4:11 KJV), and to *"humble yourselves under the mighty hand of God, that He may exalt you in due time, casting all your care upon Him, for He cares for you"* (1 Peter 5:6-7).

Remember, *"to every thing there is a season, and a time to every purpose under the heaven,"* most especially, *"A time to be born"* (Ecclesiastes 3:1-2 KJV). God is faithful, for Paul said, *"He [can be trusted] not to let you be tempted and tried and assayed beyond your ability and strength of resistance and power to endure, but...will [always] also provide the way out...that you may be capable and strong and powerful to bear up under it patiently"* (1 Corinthians 10:13 AMP). God's Word is being perfected in you and will be revealed through you at the perfect time.

> *"A woman does not give birth before she feels the pain;*
> *she does not give birth to a son before the pain starts. No*
> *one has ever heard of that happening; no one has ever seen*
> *that happen. In the same way no one ever saw a country*
> *begin in one day; no one has ever heard of a new nation*
> *beginning in one moment. But Jerusalem will give birth*
> *to her children just as soon as she feels the birth pains.*
> *In the same way I will not cause pain without allowing*
> *something new to be born,"* says the Lord. *"If I cause you*
> *the pain, I will not stop you from giving birth to your*
> *new nation,"* says your God. —Isaiah 66:7-9 NCV

If we tarry here we expect to labor in the cause of salvation and if we go hence we expect to continue our work until the coming of the Son of Man. The only difference is, while we are here we are subject to pain and sorrow, while they on the other side are free from affliction of every kind. —WILFORD WOODRUFF (1807–1898)

Chapter 5

THE MIDWIFE

Keep away from people who try to belittle your ambitions.
Small people always do that, but the really great ones make
you feel that you, too, can become great. —MARK TWAIN

Birthing is a process requiring love, trust, and support from others. When a woman is in the midst of hard labor, she not only taps into intense inner strength and tenacity, but is also at the same time intensely vulnerable. To bring forth the life she carries, to deliver and be delivered, a woman needs to be surrounded by those who are looking out for her best interests as well as believe the best of her. Author and professor of sociology Barbara Katz Rothman astutely observed, "Birth is not only about making babies. Birth is about making mothers—strong, competent, capable mothers who trust themselves and know their inner strength."[11] In the words of author and midwife

Claudia Lowe, "Only with trust, faith, and support can the woman allow the birth experience to enlighten and empower her."

In one of the most ancient and sacred books to come out of China, the *Tao Te Ching*— believed to have been published in the sixth century BC—we read this word of advice for the aspiring midwife:

> You are a midwife, assisting at someone else's birth. Do good without show or fuss. Facilitate what is happening rather than what you think ought to be happening. If you must take the lead, lead so that the mother is helped, yet still free and in charge. When the baby is born, the mother will rightly say: "We did it ourselves!"

Birth is not just about delivering something new, but also about empowering the deliverer. Midwifery, in other words, is the art of bringing out the best potential hidden deep within another. It is defined as "one who assists in or takes a part in bringing about a result."[12] It is about people working synergistically together to bring forth the divine intents and purposes God has ordained for the members of His Body.

We need to be able to recognize in one another what God has planted in each of our hearts and that our destinies are interrelated: *"As each part does its own special work, it helps the other parts grow, so that the whole body is healthy and growing and full of love"* (Ephesians 4:16 NLT). There will be occasions for me to push you and occasions for you to push me—the Body of Christ must come together to birth our God-given assignments into the earthly realm.

In essence, we are called to *midwife*, or "work together with," those who labor in bringing forth new life. A midwife is any person you bring into your life to help provide you with the emotional and spiritual resources necessary for you to safely deliver what God has given you by way of purpose and destiny. In her book, *Midwives: Pioneers of Faith*, Sarah Zadok observed, "A midwife's role, among other things, is to encourage a birthing mother to 'let go' and allow herself to become a conduit for this great Force to flow through."[13]

In 1493 a young German physician by the name of Eucharius Rösslin wrote the first widely published guidebook on the art of midwifery. In 1532 his son translated the book into Latin, and in 1540 it was translated into English. It was oddly enough entitled *The Byrth of Mankynde*, and it became the foundation for the development of the profession as we know it today. Here is a telling excerpt from the mid-sixteenth-century English translation:

> The midwife her selfe shall sit before the labouring woman, and shall diligently observe and waite, how much and after what means the child stireth itselfe. Also the midwife must instruct and comfort the party, not only refreshing her with good meate and drinke, but also with sweet words, giving her hope of a good speedie deliverance, encouraging...her to patience and tolerance.[14]

A midwife comforts, encourages, and brings hopes. She patiently "stands by" those who labor. In fact, the word *obstetrics* is derived from the Latin *obstare*, which means "to stand by." Scripture records in Genesis 35:17 the words of the midwife who stood by Rachel as she gave birth to Benjamin: *"Now it came to pass, when she was in hard labor, that the midwife said to her, 'Do not fear; you will have this son also.'"* Oftentimes, these are the most important words a midwife will use as she stands by those who find themselves disoriented by the pains of labor: "Do not fear."

There are times a midwife must encourage an expectant mother to be still and wait, to breathe deeply and stay calm. An expert midwife knows when energy is best conserved for a later time and when it is the right time to bear down and push hard. A midwife will help the mother pace herself in order to conserve her strength. We read in 2 Kings 19:3 where Hezekiah prophesied about the impending calamity of the nation of Israel not having the strength to deliver at the moment of birth: *"This day is a day of trouble, and rebuke, and blasphemy; for the children have come to birth, but there is no strength to bring them forth."*

Referring back to the mid-sixteenth-century edition of *The Byrth of Mankynde*, we read this wise admonition:

> But this must the midwife above all things take heede of, that she compell not the woman to labour before the birth come forward.... For before that time, all labour is in vaine...and in this case many times it cometh to passe, that the party hath laboured so sore before the time, that when she should labour indeed, her might and strength is spent before in vaine, so that she is not now able to helpe her selfe, and that is a perillous case.[15]

Wisdom is required not to force the issue too soon as well as to maximize every window of opportunity that presents itself. In other words, timing is everything.

Sarah Zadok, who is an expert in the Jewish tradition of midwifery, notes that "trust in the natural process of labor and in a woman's body to birth normally and safely is the hallmark of midwifery care."[16] She uses the examples of two midwives found in the Old Testament during a critical time in Israel's history. These were the famous midwives in the Book of Exodus, who turned out to be the mother and sister of Moses, Jochebed and Miriam, and who are identified as Shiphrah and Puah in Exodus 1:15. Zadok comments that these women "became God's partners in creation, granting life to the Jewish children."[17]

An article published by the *Jewish Women's Archive* states:

> It is significant that the Biblical text actually mentions
> Shifra and Puah by name, suggesting the ultimate impor-
> tance of their role in the liberation of the Israelites. The
> Talmudic sages taught that the names "Shifra" and "Puah"
> indicate different roles midwives play. "Shifra" stems from
> the Hebrew verb to swaddle or to clean a baby, while Puah
> comes from the Hebrew word to cry out because a midwife
> tries to calm a new mother's cries by offering her words of
> encouragement.[18]

Shiphrah is rooted in the Aramaic word *meshaperet,* and it means
"to make beautiful,"[19] or more literally, "to straighten."[20] The Hebrew
name *Shifra* is derived from the Hebrew root meaning, "the capacity
to make something better, or to improve its quality."[21] Interestingly
enough, *Puah* is the Hebrew word for "mouth" and comes from a
Hebrew root that implies a particular gift of speech.[22] The Aramaic
verb *po'ah* means to "cry out." This is the same word used in Isaiah
42:14: *"Now I will cry out and strain like a woman giving birth to
a child"* (NCV). "Why was her name called Puah?" asks artist and
Jewish scholar Sarah Leah Hankes. "Because she cried out [*po'ah*] to
the child and brought it forth." Hankes adds that "another explana-
tion of Puah is that she used to cry out through the Holy Spirit [the
prophetic gift] and say: 'My mother will bear a son who will be the
savior of Israel.'"[23] We can see the critical significance of the midwife's
role in bringing about "something better" and interceding on behalf
of that which is yet to be born.

Shiphrah and Puah were faithful servants of God. Because of their
obedience, the nation of Israel was fruitful and multiplied even under
the harshest of conditions. *"Therefore God dealt well with the midwives: and the people multiplied, and waxed very mighty. And it came*

to pass, because the midwives feared God, that He made them houses" (Exodus 1:20-21 KJV). The "houses" referred to here are believed to be both the priestly dynasty that came forth from Jochebed, who, being married to a Levite, bore Moses and Aaron; as well as the royal dynasty birthed through Miriam, who was married to Caleb from the tribe of Judah, and from whom sprang forth the House of David.

What is important to understand is that in our immediate environment we need people who are able to co-labor with us in bringing forth the divine potential we carry, people who are able to empower and encourage us, discern God's timing, cry out on our behalf, and be a calming and comforting force that continually draws us into the presence of God. Much as the Divine Midwife, the Holy Spirit, hovers over us to draw out the seed of promise each of us carry, we must be surrounded by a network of human supporters standing by to coach and help us breathe when we are being overcome by the pain of labor. We need to be mindful of our relationships—those we allow to speak into our lives and influence us. Has God planted an idea for a business, a book, or a ministry in your heart that perhaps you aborted because you were waiting for someone's approval? Are there abortive spirits in your midst that are on assignment to kill the deliverance God wants to birth through you?

It is important that you are careful to only allow spiritual midwives into the delivery room with you. You need God-appointed midwives. Spiritual midwifery requires a special type of kingdom practitioner who is able to skillfully apply the process and technology of intercessory prayer. Be careful that you do not allow a spiritual abortionist in the delivery room with you. Those are individuals whose negativity, doubt, unbelief, frustrations, and fears can potentially undermine and sabotage your success and prosperity.

I entreat you: discern the spirit working through the individuals in your midst. As you pray, ask God to reveal every satanic agenda and agent; ask Him to squelch demonic activities. Ask Him to frustrate the plans of the spirit of Pharaoh. Ask God to send spiritual midwives—people who will help you push past the discomfort, pain, and disappointment of an old season into the joy of the new, people who will support and cover you with their gift of speech, speaking out and interceding on your behalf. Pray for God to send those who know how to touch heaven and unlock its divine portals of grace and blessing. In the words of Sarah Zadok, "May G-d bless them to continue in the paths of Shifra and Puah, fearing G-d, not man, and through their faith in the G-dliness of birth, bless them to be His partners in creation."[24]

But the midwives had far too much respect
for God and didn't do what the king of
Egypt ordered. —EXODUS 1:17 MSG

I think of midwifery as a seed full of potential—a
seed that will grow into a lush, blossoming tree with
green branches and plenty of ripe fruit for nurturing
women, babies, and families. —MARINA ALZUGARAY

Speak tenderly to them. Let there be kindness in your
face, in your eyes, in your smile, in the warmth of your
greeting. Always have a cheerful smile. Don't only give
your care, but give your heart as well. —MOTHER TERESA

Chapter 6

PUSH

*Childbirth, perhaps more than any other life event, is an
experience that demands a strong dose of faith and surrender.
No matter how well planned or organized we may be, the
inevitable moment will arise, where the birthing woman must
face the fact that there is a force at play that is larger than
herself. As her baby moves down the narrow passage towards
birth, and contractions rush through her body with the force
of a tidal wave surging towards land, the birthing woman
is presented with a sublime choice: to faithfully submit to its
power, or to fight it tooth and nail.* —SARAH ZADOK[25]

In the final phase of the birth process, when the long hours of labor
have finally passed, and just before you feel an uncontrollable urge
to bear down and push with all of your strength to bring forth the
new life you are bursting to deliver, there is what birth practitioners

call "transition." Transition can be described as the period of time during which your body is preparing to push. Although it is the most intense time of labor, it is the shortest, lasting only fifteen to thirty minutes. It is a critical time, however, because it is when the mother is commonly overcome by an overwhelming desire to give up.

Transition is the dark before the dawn. It provides the signal that the baby has dropped into the birth canal and is positioned to come into the world. It is often the time when the mother's water will break, the time when the body is fully dilated, completely yielded, and ready to push the baby from the womb into the world. It is when the woman will exclaim she can't "do it anymore." It is not unusual during this phase that a woman will doubt her ability to go on. Transition is the time when the mother is the most emotionally needy and when her energy is physically at its lowest.

During transition, a woman must dig deep within herself to hang on. It is when the mother is for the most part soloing—the coaching offered by the midwife throughout labor will, at this point, be considered useless and even irritating. The midwife knows to keep the room quiet, instructions minimal, and communication positive. Until her guidance is needed when it is time to push, the woman in transition must lean in and trust her inner strength. Further medication is pointless because the duration of transition would not allow time for it to take effect.

Just before the urge to push takes over, the contractions subside, and activity kicks in as the mother positions herself to bear down. It is the most intimate, transparent time between a woman and her own soul—she is vulnerable. It is almost a call from God to go deep in trusting and leaning on Him, to shed every self-righteous ounce of self-will and completely give over to the Divine within. It is where the rubber meets the road when God says, *"My grace...is enough for you [sufficient against any danger and enables you to bear the trouble manfully]; for My strength and power are made perfect (fulfilled and completed) and show themselves most effective in [your] weakness."* Then Paul says, *"For when I am weak [in human strength], then am I [truly] strong (able, powerful in divine strength)"* (2 Corinthians 12:9-10 AMP).

This is when radical enlarging takes place to allow the baby to drop down and signal that it is time to begin pushing. It is when the mother must give over and *"let the power of the Master expand, enlarge itself greatly"* (Numbers 14:17 MSG) on her behalf. It is almost as if God is answering the call to *"enlarge the place of your tent, and let them stretch out the curtains of your dwellings"* (Isaiah 54:2), and as if the body is in and of itself crying out to its Maker, *"Bless me and enlarge my territory! Let Your hand be with me, and keep me from harm so that I will be free from pain!"* (1 Chronicles 4:10 NIV). To this cry God faithfully answers: *"Behold, I will do a new thing, now it shall spring forth; shall you not know it? I will even make a road in the wilderness and rivers in the desert"* (Isaiah 43:19). The mother will know exactly when that new thing is about to spring forth. If her water hasn't already broken, it will—like a river in the desert—and the baby will suddenly drop into the birth canal—the road in the wilderness—and immediately this new little being will begin to emerge, *"whose breaking comes suddenly, in an instant"* (Isaiah 30:13).

Likewise, according to Certified Nurse Midwife Peg Plumbo, prematurely initiating the pushing phase can be counterproductive and even harmful. Plumbo distinguishes between *directive pushing* and *spontaneous pushing*, stating that "most mothers should be encouraged to push when they want to push and for as long as they want to push." She suggests that a woman listens to her body, giving in to the urge to push only when it comes naturally. "Studies are now confirming what midwives have known for centuries—mothers know how to birth their babies. They don't require...a gallery of spectators to tell them, even demand them, to push."[26] In the words of birth professional Virginia Di Orio, "Just as a woman's heart knows how and when to pump, her lungs to inhale, and her hand to pull back from fire, so she knows when and how to give birth." The key to birthing—and to effectively "pushing"—is to get in tune with the natural rhythm of the body.

In *Birthing Naturally*, author Jennifer VanderLaan adds a bit of advice that throws some light on how to approach the pushing process when it comes to prayer. "If the urge to push is not strong, it may be better to change position or lean into the contraction until the pushing urge is strong. This helps to prevent fatigue and allows the strongest pushing to be done when it will be the most effective."[27] I am reminded of the time Jesus coached His disciples in Matthew 11: *"Are you tired? Worn out? Burned out? …Walk with Me and work with Me—watch how I do it. Learn the unforced rhythms of grace"* (Matthew 11:28-29 MSG). Learning to walk and work with Jesus in the "unforced rhythms of grace" might simply require you to realign or reposition yourself, to lean into the circumstances that are pressing around you, allowing them to direct your prayers rather than battling them in your own strength.

Allow faith and trust in the Lord to buoy you. Guard your heart. Paul reminds us, *"Be anxious for nothing, but in everything by prayer and supplication, with thanksgiving, let your requests be made known to God; and the peace of God, which surpasses all understanding, will guard your hearts and minds through Christ Jesus"* (Philippians 4:6-7). Philippians 4:8 goes on to talk about what kinds of thoughts you should allow to occupy your mind—*"meditate on these things…and the God of peace will be with you"* (Philippians 4:8-9). When you are pressing for your blessing, this is of vital importance. Your thought life will determine the intensity and duration of your labor.

Dr. Grantley Dick-Read was the first to explore the relationship between a woman's mindset and her ability to navigate the stormy seas of labor. He described the Fear-Tension-Pain Cycle as the overwhelming impact fear can have on a labor.[28] Fear, in other words, predisposes the mind and body to the worst possible outcome—the mind panics and the body stiffens, exponentially intensifying the pain of every contraction. The key is to relax into and work with each contraction without fighting or resisting the increasing tightening. It is the ultimate surrender. The repeated pattern of constricting forces is what is actually causing the uterus to expand.

Working with the unforced rhythms of grace may be a matter of allowing natural forces, such as gravity, to work on your behalf. Birthing positions that allow the pull of gravity to work with the rhythm of the body's contractions are the most successful. "You should become familiar with the positions that most commonly promote a healthy delivery," advises medical writer Christine Cadena. "For example, squatting may provide for a greater opportunity to work with gravity...allowing for less discomfort and greater room for your baby to move."[29]

Likewise, when you pray, posture yourself in ways that will allow you to best connect with how the Spirit is moving—whether you kneel, stand, or lay flat on the ground—be willing to adjust your position. You have the power to align yourself with the currents of God's grace just as a birthing mother aligns her body with the pull of gravity. Dr. John H. Kennell advocated, "One of the best things we could do would be to help women/parents/families discover their own birth power, from within themselves. And to let them know it's always been there, they just need to tap into it."[30]

Birthing pools are also used to ease the transition phase and expedite the pushing process. Gentle, natural, and supportive, these pools offer a calming environment that undergirds the birthing mother while at the same time providing the newborn a peaceful transition into the natural world. The infant birthed underwater emerges into the welcoming environment of a bath imbued with the soothing sounds of music. Similarly, after we travail in prayer, there should be a time of the washing of the water of the Word in an atmosphere of praise and worship. This should be a part of our own birthing process as we enter anew into the kingdom of God each and every day.

Similar to the practice of New Testament baptism in signifying conversion and the "new birth," Jewish women renew their reproductive rites each month by submersing in the "living waters" of the *mikvah*. The word *mikvah* literally means "a collection of living waters" and is designated for the sole purpose of purification and renewal. The Hebrew root of this word is loosely translated to mean "hope."[31] Each month, Hebrew women go through a spiritual and physical cleansing before immersing themselves in the "living waters" of the *mikvah*. It is believed to keep the marriage relationship pure and vibrant. Like the birthing pool, the *mikvah* offers a soothing and invigorating rebirth with every new cycle. In the words of Christopher Largen, "Birth is an experience that demonstrates that life is not merely function and utility, but form and beauty."

The intense time of travail, transition, and at last pushing forth life is one of capacity building, enlarging, strengthening, and purifying. It is a time of letting go and pressing forth, a time of surrender and perseverance. In the words of author David Hammarskjold, "Life only demands from you the strength you possess." As conveyers of the life of God, you can be assured that God's grace is always more than enough (2 Corinthians 12:9 AMP, MSG, and NCV).

Yet You brought me safely from my mother's womb and led me to trust You at my mother's breast. I was thrust into Your arms at my birth. You have been my God from the moment I was born. —Psalm 22:9-10 NLT

When you have come to the edge
of all the light you know
And are about to step off
Into the darkness of the unknown,
Faith is knowing that
One of two things will happen:
There will be something solid to stand on
Or you will be taught how to fly. —Patrick Overter

The Wombs of
Heaven and Earth

GIVING BIRTH TO
GOD'S DIVINE PLAN

Chapter 7

THE MIND OF GOD

*I want to know God's thoughts...the rest
are details.* —ALBERT EINSTEIN

*"My thoughts are nothing like your thoughts," says the
Lord. "And My ways are far beyond anything you could
imagine. For just as the heavens are higher than the earth,
so My ways are higher than your ways and My thoughts
higher than your thoughts."* —ISAIAH 55:8-9 NLT

Throughout my life I have undertaken a variety of ambitious goals. My quest to know more about God carried me along twisting and winding turns within spiritual realms I never knew existed. At times I imagined what Christopher Columbus might have felt as he journeyed into the unknown attempting to discover a new world which he could only speculate existed beyond the horizon.

My journey into the unfathomable mind of God unfolded with unexpected yet tantalizing mysteries of the Spirit. It was fraught with as much intrigue and excitement as frustration and uncertainty because the horizon continued to expand. As question after question flooded my mind, it created a paradoxical tension summed up in the following question: "How does one with finite intelligence explain the infinite, all-knowing, all-powerful God—let alone His mind?"

My own mind began down a familiar path of reasoning. "If there is a created thing, then certainly there must be a creator of that thing. Accordingly, if there is a creator, then the intents and purposes of that creator will be hidden within the mind of that creator." I reasoned that if words are thoughts clothed in language, then the words spoken by God would hold the encrypted keys to unlocking the door of His mind.

In the first chapter of Genesis we are told that God created humankind in His image and after His likeness (Genesis 1:26). God created humans to be thinking beings capable of anticipating and altering events to suit a desired outcome—because that is the kind of being God is. If everything that exists in the world emanated from the mind and imagination of God, then we can surmise that the personal world we each experience must therefore emanate from our own minds and imaginations as well.

Additionally, if God created this world with purpose and meaning, we can be confident He created us with purpose and meaning as well. Moreover, God has given each of us the means by which we can tap into His mind in order to discover that purpose—that means is called prayer.

Prayer is simply communicating with God and allowing Him to communicate with you. Through prayer we are given the opportunity to know the mind of God. Prayer is somewhat like hacking into the mainframe of a master computer. A hacker knows which keys to hit and commands to give in order to extract information that the average person has no idea how to access.

The great innovator George Washington Carver put it this way: "I love to think of nature as an unlimited broadcasting system through which God speaks to us every hour, if we will only tune in."[32] He added this observation about his own ability to create: "I never have to grope for methods. The method is revealed at the moment I am inspired to create something new. Without God to draw aside the curtain I would be helpless."[33] David said it like this in Psalm 19, *"The heavens declare the glory of God, and the sky above proclaims His handiwork. Day to day pours out speech, and night to night reveals knowledge. There is no speech, nor are there words, whose voice is not heard"* (Psalm 19:1-3 ESV).

The great patriarch Abraham used prayer to tap into the mind of God. In Genesis 18, we read about God's anger against the prevailing sinfulness of Sodom and Gomorrah. Learning of God's forthcoming wrath, Abraham gets into God's head, asking if He would destroy the good people along with the sinners: *"Then Abraham drew near and said, 'Will You indeed sweep away the righteous with the wicked? Suppose there are fifty righteous within the city. Will You then sweep away the place and not spare it for the fifty righteous who are in it?'"* (Genesis 18:23-24 ESV). Abraham was getting into the mind of God when he reasoned, *"Far be it from You to do such a thing, to put the righteous to death with the wicked, so that the righteous fare as the wicked! Far be that from You! Shall not the Judge of all the earth do what is just?"* (Genesis 18:25 ESV). And the Lord conceded, *"I will spare the whole place for their sake.... For the sake of ten I will not destroy it"* (Genesis 18:26,32 ESV).

From this text we understand that God had a plan in mind. Abraham was able to tap into God's mind through prayer. Prayer is the vehicle that allows you to access the mind of God so you can determine His will for any given situation, but most especially for your life. He has a plan and a future in mind for you, an expected end that is for your good and never a surprise to Him. He begins every story with the end in mind!

A favorite illustration of mine was told to me by one of my staff members. It goes something like this:

> A man was sleeping one night in his cabin when suddenly his room filled with light and God appeared. The Lord told the man He had work for him to do and showed him a large rock in front of his cabin. The Lord explained that the man was to push against the rock with all his might. So this the man did, day after day.
>
> For many years the man toiled from sunup to sundown, his shoulders set squarely against the cold, massive surface of the unmoving rock, pushing with all of his might. Each night the man returned to his cabin sore and worn out, feeling that his whole day had been spent in vain.
>
> Seeing that the man was showing signs of discouragement, the Adversary decided to enter the picture by placing thoughts into the man's weary mind: "You've been pushing against that rock for a long time, and it hasn't budged. Why kill yourself over this? You're never going to move it"—thus, giving the man the impression that the task was impossible and that he was a failure. These thoughts discouraged and disheartened the man.
>
> "Why kill myself over this?" he thought. "I'll just put in my time, giving just the minimum effort and that'll be good

enough." And that's just what he planned to do—until one day he decided to make it a matter of prayer and take his troubled thoughts to the Lord. "Lord," he said, "I've labored long and hard in Your service, putting all my strength to do that which You've asked. Yet, after all this time, I haven't even budged that rock by half a millimeter. What's wrong? Why am I failing?"

The Lord responded compassionately: "My friend, when I asked you to serve Me—you accepted. I told you that your task was to push against the rock with all your strength—which you've done. Never once did I mention to you that I expected you to move it. Your task was to push. And now you come to Me with your strength spent, thinking that you've failed. But is that really so?

"Look at yourself. Your arms are strong and muscular. Your back sinew is mighty. Your hands are callused from the constant pressure, and your legs have become massive and hard. Through opposition you've grown much and your abilities now surpass that which you used to have. Yet you haven't moved the rock. But your calling was to be obedient and to push and to exercise your faith and trust in My wisdom. This you've done. I, My friend, will now move the rock."[34]

God did not move the rock until the man had pushed long and hard enough over the course of time and sought Him through prayer. He had to build "prayer muscles" before he was able to move the hand of God—and even then it was God who answered and moved on his behalf. Sometimes when we attempt to discern the purpose, plans, and will of God, it may feel as if we are attempting to do the impossible. But keep on pushing in prayer and God will answer.

Jesus told His disciples that persistence in prayer pays off. He shared with them a parable of a man coming to a friend's house late at night to ask for a loaf of bread. The friend would not answer the door because he had already gone to bed, *"yet because of his persistence he will rise and give him as many as he needs"* (Luke 11:8). The lesson, Jesus went on to explain, is this: *"So I say to you, ask, and it will be given to you; seek, and you will find; knock, and it will be opened to you. For everyone who asks receives, and he who seeks finds, and to him who knocks it will be opened"* (Luke 11:9-10).

God wants nothing but your good. He wants you to be exercised and strengthened spiritually. He wants you to learn to trust Him and for your faith to continually grow, like a mustard seed that *"grows up and becomes greater than all herbs, and shoots out large branches, so that the birds of the air may nest under its shade"* (Mark 4:32). God wants to take you from glory to glory as you increasingly lean on and trust in His goodness. The Lord told Jeremiah, *"For I know the plans I have for you...plans for good and not for disaster, to give you a future and a hope.... When you pray, I will listen. If you look for Me wholeheartedly, you will find Me"* (Jeremiah 29:11-13 NLT).

At times when we hear a word from God, we tend to use our own intellect to decipher what He wants, when actually what God wants is just simple obedience and faith in Him. By all means, exercise the faith that moves mountains, but know that it is still God who moves the mountains.

> ***And whatever things you ask in prayer, believing, you will receive. —MATTHEW 21:22***

Chapter 8

CHRIST

We faintly hear, we dimly see,
In differing phrase we pray;
But dim or clear, we own in Him
The life, the truth, the way.
—JOHN GREENLEAF WHITTIER

"What mist hath dimmed that glorious face! / What seas of grief my sun doth toss! / The golden rays of heavenly grace / Lies now eclipsed upon the cross,"[35] wrote an English priest named Robert Southwell before being martyred in 1595. Indeed, as Jesus hung on the cross breathing His last mortal breaths, the world experienced a total eclipse of the sun: *"The whole earth became dark, the darkness lasting three hours—a total blackout"* (Luke 23:44 MSG). The ground shook, the earth grew dark, and the temple curtain was torn from top to bottom (Matthew 27:45.) *"Jesus groaned out of the depths"* (Mark 15:33 MSG) as He cried out. Something momentous was happening in both the heavens and the earth. A new entity was being brought forth from the spiritual realm into the temporal realm—a literal earth-shattering event.

As Mary travailed to birth the "Word made flesh" (John 1) into the earth, now Jesus travailed as He brought forth what would become His Body in the earth—the Church. For three hours the earth was dark before the Lord commended His Spirit to God. Afterward, His side was pierced *"so that the scripture would be fulfilled...'They will look on the One they have pierced'"* (John 19:36-37 NIV). And as there is both blood and water involved in the birth of a child, there was both blood and water that came forth from Jesus, birthing the Church: *"One of the soldiers pierced His side with a spear, and immediately blood and water came out"* (John 19:34). Jesus birthed the Church there on the cross. The Bride of Christ was taken from His side even as Eve was taken from the rib of Adam.

Christ brought the Church forth from His own being—He created it in His likeness to function as He functioned in the earth. As He was the Word made flesh when He walked among us two thousand years ago, so is the Church God's Word made flesh in the world today. At the same time, as a husband and wife are *"one flesh—no longer two bodies but one"* (Matthew 19:4 MSG), so are Christ and the Church now one body. In comparing the relationship of Christ and the Church to that of a marriage, Paul explained it in this way to the Ephesians:

> *Christ's love makes the church whole. His words evoke her beauty. Everything He does and says is designed to bring the best out of her, dressing her in dazzling white silk, radiant with holiness. And that is how husbands ought to*

love their wives. They're really doing themselves a favor—since they're already "one" in marriage.

No one abuses his own body, does he? No, he feeds and pampers it. That's how Christ treats us, the church, since we are part of His body. And this is why a man leaves father and mother and cherishes his wife. No longer two, they become "one flesh" (Ephesians 5:26-31 MSG).

Jesus prayed to His Father in heaven, *"The same glory You gave Me, I gave them, so they'll be as unified and together as We are—I in them and You in Me. Then they'll be mature in this oneness, and give the godless world evidence that You've sent Me and loved them in the same way You've loved Me"* (John 17:22-23 MSG). We, who are born of God, are one with Christ. We have come forth from His body to be His Body—we are *"the assembly of God's firstborn children"* (Hebrews 12:23 NLT).

> *Near, so very near to God,*
> *Nearer I cannot be;*
> *For in the person of His Son I am as near as He.*
> *So dear, so very dear to God,*
> *More dear I cannot be;*
> *The love wherewith He loves the Son—*
> *Such is His love to me. —CATESBY PAGET*

We, "the Church of the firstborn," are heirs of God and joint-heirs with Christ. We are made in His image to reflect His glory (1 Corinthians 11:7). As the Body of Christ, we are empowered by the Holy Spirit, the *Spirit of Life*, the genesis of all. Christ breathed that Spirit into the Church giving it life just as God breathed life into the first man He formed from the dust of the ground so that he *"became a living being"* (Genesis 2:7 AMP). Paul wrote to the

Romans, *"A new power is in operation."* He explained that the *"Spirit of life in Christ, like a strong wind, has magnificently cleared the air, freeing you from a fated lifetime of brutal tyranny at the hands of sin and death"* (Romans 8:2 MSG).

The Church in the earth, birthed forth from the agony and passion of Christ, is His living will and testament; it is His Word alive in the world today. We are a living testimony to the power of God. We are called to overcome the world, to *"overcome evil with good"* (Romans 12:21). Jesus told His disciples that whoever was born of Him—whoever trusted and believed on Him—would do far greater things than even He did.

> *Believe Me: I am in My Father and My Father is in Me. If you can't believe that, believe what you see—these works. The person who trusts Me will not only do what I'm doing but even greater things, because I, on My way to the Father, am giving you the same work to do that I've been doing. You can count on it. From now on, whatever you request along the lines of who I am and what I am doing, I'll do it. That's how the Father will be seen for who He is in the Son. I mean it. Whatever you request in this way, I'll do* (John 14:11-14 MSG).

The Church is Christ's legacy, His Body alive in the earth today. If we fail to grow in that role, we have simply *"lost connection with the Head, from whom the whole body, supported and held together by its ligaments and sinews, grows as God causes it to grow"* (Colossians 2:19 NIV). Don't become dismembered from His Body. Stay connected.

But we know that there is only one God, the Father, who created everything, and we live for Him. And there is only one Lord, Jesus Christ, through whom God made everything and through whom we have been given life. —1 CORINTHIANS 8:6 NLT

It concerns Him who, being the holiest among the mighty, and the mightiest among the holy, lifted with His pierced hands empires off their hinges, turned the stream of centuries out of its channels, and still governs the ages. —JEAN PAUL RICHTER

Chapter 9

THE CHURCH

You come with a birthright, written in love and sung
through all Creation in words which promise
that no matter where you're at, you're home
that no matter who you're with, you're welcome
that no matter who you are, you're loved.
Welcome. —Rita Ramsey

You have come to the assembly of God's firstborn children,
whose names are written in heaven. You have come to
God Himself, who is the judge over all things. You have
come to the spirits of the righteous ones in heaven who
have now been made perfect. —Hebrews 12:23 NLT

Many of us have been undermined by a world system that is not constructed for liberty, but in such a way that it brings about victimization and a misuse of our abilities and talents—our anointings and mantels—much like what happened with the prodigal son in Luke 15. The Bible tells us this son went into the world system and wasted his substance—his gifts, his talents, and his time—*"he wasted everything he had"* (Luke 15:13 MSG)—and when the world got through with him, it abandoned him to the realm of the pigs. We read how in desperation the son *"went and joined himself to a citizen of that country, and he sent him into his fields to feed swine"* (Luke 15:15). And even then, *"He would have been glad to eat what the pigs were eating, but no one gave him a thing"* (Luke 15:16 CEV).

When he came to himself, he went back to his father's house where he was received, restored, and reestablished as a son and heir. His father clothed him with new shoes and a robe and placed a ring upon his finger. This is a beautiful illustration of how the Father receives us when we return home to Him.

> *And he arose and came to his father. But when he was still a great way off, his father saw him and had compassion, and ran and fell on his neck and kissed him. And the son said to him, "Father, I have sinned against heaven and in your sight, and am no longer worthy to be called your son."*
>
> *But the father said to his servants, "Bring out the best robe and put it on him, and put a ring on his hand and sandals on his feet. And bring the fatted calf here and kill it, and let us eat and be merry; for this my son was dead and is alive again; he was lost and is found." And they began to be merry* (Luke 15:20-24).

In the world, the Church is our Father's house. It is a place where our heavenly Father puts new shoes on our feet and wraps a robe around our shoulders. I believe the shoes speak of affluence, the robe speaks of our mantels of anointing, and the ring represents our authority. When you are walking in your true authority and fully functioning in your area of anointing, it is only then that you become the leader, influencer, and contributing member of society that God has ordained you to be.

God wants to bring you into a place of dominion where you are proactive in your life based on the vision and plans and purposes God has predestined for you. The Church should be a place that matures us. The role of the Church is to grow us up in Christ—to make us emotionally mature, socially congruent, spiritually stable, and economically savvy. Why? It is so *that we should no longer be children, tossed to and fro and carried about with every wind of doctrine, by the trickery of men, in the cunning craftiness of deceitful plotting,"* but instead we would *"grow up in all things into Him who is the head— Christ—from whom the whole body, joined and knit together by what every joint supplies, according to the effective working by which every part does its share, causes growth of the body for the edifying of itself in love"* (Ephesians 4:14-16).

Some of you may not have come from the best home or have the best family, but in Christ you are made perfect. When you are grafted into the Body of Christ, you are truly born again as an entirely new creation (2 Corinthians 5:17). God has a new home and a second chance for you. If your first home did not give you everything you needed to be happy, healthy, and successful in every way, when you come into the house of God you are given a new home, a new family, and a new Father. Jehovah is your adopted Father—and the longer you hang out with Him the more you become like Him. He welcomes you with an embrace and a kiss, and He places His robe around your shoulders and His ring on your hand. You are His child.

Being adopted into the family of God is different from being adopted into a natural family. In a natural family, unless there is a fluke of nature, you will not look like your adoptive parents. You might have some resemblance to them, but you won't ever look exactly like your adoptive great-grandmother or cousin or aunt. However, when you are adopted into the family of God, you will grow to look exactly like your heavenly Father. *"It has not yet been revealed what we shall be, but we know that when He is revealed, we shall be like Him"* (1 John 3:2). There is a genetic transformation that takes place—a change of genotype and phenotype.

The genotype determines your phenotype—what you look like on the outside. To be regenerated has the connotation of being "re-gened" right down to your spiritual DNA. By changing us genetically in the realm of the spirit, God was the first to successfully practice bioengineering.

God is in the business of regeneration. He "re-genes" us and causes us to be born again and delivered into a new realm. It doesn't matter how you started out, what matters is who God has in mind for you to be; what matters is how you finish.

Through His Church, which is His Body in the earth, God is birthing us. We are delivered when we go from one spiritual dimension to another, from the realm of the kingdom of darkness to the realm of the kingdom of light. In the classical Pentecostal church, we call it "being delivered" when someone receives freedom from demonic oppression, possession, or a sinful bondage. But if you look at deliverance from another perspective—such as when a baby is delivered from the dark confines of the womb into the light of the open air, so it is when you receive the light of revelation through the five-fold ministry gifts. You experience a form of deliverance when you are *"being transformed into the same image from glory to glory, just as by the Spirit of the Lord"* (2 Corinthians 3:18).

This is our deliverance. Through the spiritual formation and maturing of every member of the Church, which is achieved through the ministries of pastors, teachers, apostles, and prophets, our true identities in Christ are being birthed. We are being called out. Interestingly, the English word *church* is derived from the Greek noun *ecclesia,* which literally means a "calling out" of citizens or a "called-out assembly." An *ecclesia* is commonly defined as "a gathering of the called-out ones."[36]

The Church is responsible for giving birth to citizens of the kingdom of heaven. Once someone accepts Christ and joins the local church, that church is then responsible for forming that new believer into heaven's ambassador—taking them beyond church membership to kingdom citizenship to heavenly ambassadorship. In the nineteenth century, Prime Minister of England and literary figure Benjamin Disraeli was quoted to have said, "Man is a being born to believe. And if no church comes forward with its title deeds of truth to guide him, he will find altars and idols in his own heart and his own imagination."

The goal of the Church should be to create globally conscious citizens committed to changing the trajectory of their nations and the destiny of their world by the power of the Holy Spirit. Every member of the Body must grow up to take responsibility, ownership, and finally dominion over the ungodly kingdoms and strongholds holding sway around the globe. This is what God purposed to accomplish through Christ—that the Church would *grow up in all things* and be empowered to take back dominion and reign in the earth through Him.

To make all see what is the fellowship of the mystery, which from the beginning of the ages has been hidden in God who created all things through Jesus Christ; to the intent that now the manifold wisdom of God might be made known by the church to the principalities and powers in the heavenly places, according to the eternal purpose which He accomplished in Christ Jesus our Lord. —EPHESIANS 3:9-11

Church isn't where you meet. Church isn't a building. Church is what you do. Church is who you are. Church is the human outworking of the person of Jesus Christ. Let's not go to Church, let's be the Church. —BRIDGET WILLARD

To the church of God...to those who are sanctified in Christ Jesus, called to be saints, with all who in every place call on the name of Jesus Christ our Lord, both theirs and ours: Grace to you and peace from God our Father and the Lord Jesus Christ. —1 CORINTHIANS 1:2-3

Chapter 10

THE EARTH

Earth is crammed with heaven
And every bush aflame with God
But only those who see take off their shoes.
—ELIZABETH BARRETT BROWNING

I want creation to penetrate you with so much admiration
that wherever you go, the least plant may bring you
the clear remembrance of the Creator.... One blade
of grass or one speck of dust is enough to occupy your
entire mind in beholding the art with which it has
been made. —ST. BASIL THE GREAT (329–379)

In the beginning, God impregnated the earth when He caused His Spirit to hover over it. We know from Genesis 1:2 that the earth started out *"without form and void"* (ESV). In the same verse we read that the *"Spirit of God was hovering over the face of the waters."* The word used here for "hover" is the same word we read in Luke when the Spirit of God "hovered" over Mary, causing her to conceive: *"The Holy Spirit will come upon you, the power of the Highest hover over you; therefore, the child you bring to birth will be called Holy, Son of God"* (Luke 1:35 MSG). Isaiah prophesied of Jesus that *"the life-giving Spirit of God will hover over Him, the Spirit that brings wisdom and understanding, The Spirit that gives direction and builds strength, the Spirit that instills knowledge and Fear-of-God"* (Isaiah 11:1-2 MSG). And in Isaiah 31:5 God declares, *"Yes, I'll hover and deliver"* (MSG).

From the outset, God, by the power of His Spirit, hovered over creation in order to bring forth life. Nothing was created that was not first imbued with God's own life sired by His Spirit. The spermatozoa of God's Word inseminated the earth that was formerly *"without form and void,"* hovering over the womb of creation, or the *"face of the deep"* (Genesis 1:1-2 ESV). God spoke and said, *"'Let there be light,' and there was light"* (Genesis 1:3 ESV). We know that it was God's Word—even Christ—that brought everything that is into being. John 1:1-3 tells us that *"In the beginning was the Word, and the Word was with God, and the Word was God. He was in the beginning with God. All things were made through him, and without him was not any thing made that was made"* (ESV).

Creation has yet to be fully delivered. In Romans Paul wrote, *"All around us we observe a pregnant creation"* (Romans 8:22 MSG). We have yet to see God's glory carried to full term. Creation, like an expectant mother, is waiting *"in eager expectation for the sons of God to be revealed"* (Romans 8:19 NIV). Paul went on to add, *"Creation looks forward to the day when it will join God's children in glorious freedom from death and decay. For we know that all creation has been groaning as in the pains of childbirth right up to the present time"* (Romans 8:21 NLT).

All that exists in the earthly realm responds to the voice of God, the Father of all creation. When God releases His Word into the womb of the earth, He germinates His purpose and sets in motion a type of mitosis that cannot be reversed. He said through the prophet Isaiah, *"My word that goes out from My mouth: it will not return to Me empty, but will accomplish what I desire and achieve the purpose for which I sent it"* (Isaiah 55:11 NIV). The voice of God produces its assignment in a set time and season. Even now the earth is forming gold and silver and pearls, oil and metals and minerals, oxygen and water and wind, continually supplying what we need for life. It seems as if no matter how much humanity extracts from the earth, it always brings forth an abundance of resources. I think of Isaiah 66:11: *"For you will nurse and be satisfied at her comforting breasts; you will drink deeply and delight in her overflowing abundance"* (NIV).

Everything that is—all we see, are, and have—started from a seed. Not only plant and animal life, but all of the earth's resources began in seed form. Rain is birthed from seeds, or dust particles, in the womb of a cloud; pearls are birthed from grains of sand in the womb of an oyster; a diamond is birthed from coal in the depths of a mine; while coal is birthed from the seeds of fossilized vegetation in the womb of the earth's crust. God proclaimed through Isaiah, *"Let the earth hear, and all that is in it, the world, and all that comes out of it!"* (Isaiah 34:1 NIV). Even man was birthed from *"the dust of the ground"* (Genesis 2:7). You never need to be intimidated because of your past—everybody comes from dirt!

All of creation is a testimony of God's redemptive, regenerative, resurrection power. It is God who makes *"everything beautiful in its time"* (Ecclesiastes 3:11). In the words of author and evangelist Kevin Graham Ford, "No matter how hard we try, we cannot separate God's work of creation and His work of redemption. Paul makes it perfectly clear the Logos, Jesus as wisdom personified, is the force behind both redemption and creation." It was the great reformer Martin Luther who profoundly stated, "God writes the Gospel, not in the Bible alone, but also on trees, and in the flowers and clouds and stars." And it was Paul the apostle who so poignantly wrote:

> For since the creation of the world God's invisible qualities—His eternal power and divine nature—have been clearly seen, being understood from what has been made, so that men are without excuse (Romans 1:20 NIV).

All of creation points to the glory and majesty of God. And just as God spoke forth all of creation, so creation speaks forth of God. It is pregnant with His purpose, provision, and redemptive power. The earth is renewed day by day, regenerated by the power of God's Spirit. Even as the Spirit awakens our understanding to His will each morning (Isaiah 50:4 NLT), so the Spirit of God awakens the earth to bring forth His purpose each new day. The psalmist understood the life-giving power of the Spirit of God when he wrote:

> What a wildly wonderful world, God! You made it all, with Wisdom at Your side, made earth overflow with Your wonderful creations.... Take back Your Spirit and they die, revert to original mud; send out Your Spirit and they spring to life—the whole countryside in bloom and blossom (Psalm 104:24,29 MSG).

God created the earth for man—and man from the earth—that he might regulate and be sustained by the earth. All the treasures in the universe come directly or indirectly from the earth. Second Corinthians 4:7 speaks of God's treasures being found in earthen vessels. Although Paul is referring to our human self as this earthen vessel, the earth is also a vessel of God's treasures. A vessel is much like a womb in that it channels the life of God in every conceivable form—and those we have yet to conceive.

There is an entire reproductive symphony that is playing through-out the universe. We see it in the animal kingdom and in the anatomical kingdom, and in the atomic and subatomic kingdoms. Creation is in a continual process of birth and regeneration. The whole earth is birthing all of the time, showing forth the resurrection power of God. *"The glory of God—let it last forever! Let God enjoy His creation!"* (Psalm 104:31 MSG).

> *Some people, in order to discover God, read books. But there is a great book: the very appearance of created things. Look above you! Look below you! Read it. God, whom you want to discover, never wrote that book with ink. Instead He set before your eyes the things that He had made. Can you ask for a louder voice than that?* —St. Augustine (354-430)

> *The heavens declare the glory of God; the skies proclaim the work of His hands. Day after day they pour forth speech; night after night they display knowledge. There is no speech or language where their voice is not heard. Their voice goes out into all the earth, their words to the ends of the world.* —Psalm 19:1-4 NIV

> *The whole earth is a living icon of the face of God.... I do not worship matter. I worship the Creator of matter who became matter for my sake, who willed to take His abode in matter, who worked out my salvation through matter. Never will I cease honoring the matter which wrought my salvation! I honor it, but not as God. Because of this I salute all remaining matter with reverence, because God has filled it with His grace and power. Through it my salvation has come to me.* —St. John of Damascus (675–749)

Chapter 11

A NATION

A nation, like a person, has a mind—a mind that must
be kept informed and alert, that must know itself, that
understands the hopes and needs of its neighbors—all
the other nations that live within the narrowing circle
of the world. —FRANKLIN DELANO ROOSEVELT

God has a placed a distinct destiny and redemptive purpose within the womb of every nation. Each nation on earth has been imprinted with a particular God-given DNA and carries the genes of its own unique identity from generation to generation. "You who are wise must know, that different nations have different conceptions," an Onondaga Indian named Canasatego told an English colonial official in 1744.

A nation is more than an area of land which lies within a set of boundaries, but it is the sum total of the hopes, disappointments, values, and beliefs of its people. As the British actor Anthony Quayle astutely observed, "To understand a man, you must know his memories. The same is true of a nation." And in the words of former U.S. President James Garfield, "Territory is but the body of a nation. The people who inhabit its hills and valleys are its soul, its spirit, its life."

The womb of a nation brings forth people who change the course of its history. It is not nations that impact history as much as the people who are born of them. God impregnates each nation with specific people—individuals He causes to come forth at specific times in history. Acts 17:26 states, *"From one man He made every nation of men, that they should inhabit the whole earth; and He determined the times set for them and the exact places where they should live"* (NIV). There isn't anything on the earth that is conceived by accident. God has put His seed into the womb of every nation and preordained that each would deliver and fulfill its purpose at an appointed time. God asked through the prophet Isaiah, *"Has a nation ever been born in a single day? Would I ever bring this nation to the point of birth and then not deliver it?"* (Isaiah 66:8-9 NLT).

God reaches into each nation and pulls forth the gift each was created to deliver. From ancient Greece came poets and philosophers; from ancient Rome came military strategists; from Italy came great painters and sculptors; from England great playwrights; from Spain explorers, from Germany reformers, from France revolutionaries, from America pioneers and industrialists; from Asia innovative managers and technologists; and from India pace-setting entrepreneurs and activists. *"This is the plan, planned for the whole earth, and this is the hand that will do it, reaching into every nation.... His is the hand that's reached out. Who could brush it aside?"* (Isaiah 14:26-27 MSG).

Martin Luther King, Jr. posed this idea: "The question is not whether we will be extremists, but what kind of extremists we will be? …The nation and the world are in dire need of creative extremists."

Mahatma Gandhi was one such creative extremist. Born in Porbandar, India on October 2, 1869, he turned the modern world on its ear. The very mention of the name "Gandhi" has become synonymous with the concept of peaceful resistance and nonviolent change. He was the father of independence and cottage industry, uniting a culturally diverse India, liberating her from British rule, and bringing the hope of self-sufficiency to the poorest of her poor. He famously stated, "We must be the change we wish to see."[37] He was also quoted as having said, "The best way to find yourself is to lose yourself in the service of others." He believed in freedom and truth and wrote, "The only tyrant I accept in this world is the still voice within," and, "Man cannot be untruthful, cruel, or incontinent and claim to have God on his side."

God positions people in a nation to bring light and revelation, to reveal Himself to the world. Like Christ, each person in Christ He *"has prepared for all people. He is a light to reveal God to the nations"* (Luke 2:31-32 NLT). It's as if God is saying to the world, *"Draw in close now, nations. Listen carefully, you people. Pay attention!"* (Isaiah 34:1 MSG). God is speaking to the nations through the people He brings forth out of those nations. Gandhi said, "My life is my message."

Nations give rise to leaders, thinkers, artists, and activists who propel the eternal purposes of God forward. Each is born into a specific nation at a specific time for a specific reason. All are called to give an account of the message they have been given to share. For example: Italy gave us Marcus Arellius; Canada gave us Aimee Semple McPherson; The Netherlands gave us Van Gogh; South Africa gave us Nelson Mandela; England gave us Sir Winston Churchill; Corsica gave us Napoleon Bonaparte; India gave us Gandhi, and Jerusalem gave us Jesus. There is no one too small, too poor, too lost, or too privileged to escape the call. Every voice counts. The eternity God has placed in every heart can have a profound impact on the course of a nation. As Queen Elizabeth II once said, "The upward course of a nation's history is due in the long run to the soundness of heart of its average men and women."[38]

What course is your nation on? How is it being directed by the condition of your own heart? What is the message God has created you to be? Can you discern the time and season in which He has positioned you—and the nation in which He has incubated you?

> *He changes the times and the seasons; He*
> *removes kings and raises up kings; He gives*
> *wisdom to the wise and knowledge to those*
> *who have understanding.* —DANIEL 2:21

> *It may be long before the law of love will be recognized*
> *in international affairs. The machineries of government*
> *stand between and hide the hearts of one people*
> *from those of another.* —MAHATMA GANDHI

The Wombs of Being

GIVING BIRTH TO WHO YOU ARE

Chapter 12

THE MALE LOINS

The seed is a gateway through which the future possibility of the living tree emerges. —PETER SENGE

Within the loins of a man lies the seed of all future possibility. The male loins carry the hope of all human potential. In many ways, you are who you are because of who your father was. Even though the woman carries the baby, it is the seed of the man that determines the child's gender and genetic blueprint; it is the father who carries within his loins some of the most important determining factors for every human being.

We are each divinely ordered. We originated from a single seed among possible millions, each racing, fighting through the crowd and breaking through the barrier between eternal oblivion and divine procreation. We end up as the seed that beat out every other seed for the sacred prize called life. We are the result of the power inherent in a singular seed to survive and succeed against all odds. This speaks to me of our resiliency as individuals. None of us would be here if it weren't for that intrinsic resiliency. The seed from which we emerged actually carries within it a generative power that reaches beyond a single lifetime, extending forth from former and beyond future generations.

It is from the seed of man that nations are birthed. From a single seed springs forth not only an entire nation but also multiple nations. Look at Abraham. God promised Abraham that He would make him a great nation, but three great nations were actually born from Abraham's seed. From the seed born of Sarah came Isaac, who became the nation of Israel; from the seed born of Hagar came Ishmael, who became the nation of Islam; and from Keturah, whom Abraham married after Sarah died, came the Assyrians, Persians, and Midianites.[39]

Later on, these nations are represented in the prophetic vision of Isaiah where he proclaimed, "Herds of camels will cover your land, young camels of Midian and Ephah. And all from Sheba will come, bearing gold and incense and proclaiming the praise of the Lord" (Isaiah 60:6 NIV). We know from Genesis 25 that Midian was Keturah's son and Ephah was Midian's son. We also read in that passage that Sheba was Keturah's grandson by her son Jokshan. In the end, there will be one epic family reunion of all the descendents of Abraham.

Abraham was faithful to the call of God upon his life. It was through his obedience that his descendents were blessed and multiplied. One man's seed determined the destiny of generations, a lineage extending from Genesis through Isaiah all the way to those born of the Spirit in Christ.

It is the father who prays, obeys, and establishes a covering over his descendents. The man provides an inheritance not only materially, but he also sets forth a vision and direction, a course in terms of values, attitudes, faithfulness, and honor. We understand from Genesis 26:18 that a righteous man establishes intergenerational blessings and wells of prosperity: *"And Isaac dug again the wells of water which they had dug in the days of Abraham his father."*

All that you and I are today is a direct result of the blessings, or the lack of them, set in motion by our forefathers. There is supernatural empowerment in generational blessings, as well as a supernatural bondage inherent in generational curses. You must pray for discernment and in Christ take authority over any disorders passed down through your family's spiritual heritage. You can do spiritual gene therapy and reorder, or realign, your life in Christ. You can stand firm as Joshua did when he challenged Israel to make a choice: *"Choose today whom you will serve...the gods your ancestors served...or will it be the gods...in whose land you now live? But as for me and my family, we will serve the Lord"* (Joshua 24:15 NLT).

What you do today will affect generations to come. I recently read a study on nutrition that discovered our health is affected in part by what our grandmothers ate two and three generations before we were even born! If this is reflected in our bodies, how much more will we see this reflected spiritually? It is not only within the power of the man, but it is his primary responsibility as the head of his household to pray for a covering over his wife, his children, and his children's children—down to the fourth generation.

We read in Numbers 14:18, *"The Lord is longsuffering and abundant in mercy, forgiving iniquity and transgression; but He by no means clears the guilty, visiting the iniquity of the fathers on the children to the third and fourth generation."* On the other hand, in 2 Kings 10:30 we read, *"Because you have done well in accomplishing what is right in My eyes...your descendants will sit on the throne of Israel to the fourth generation"* (NIV). Interestingly enough, according to biblical numerics, four is the number of completion.

The future of your seed requires a covering in prayer. Just as the skin covers the body, the ozone layer covers the earth, the roof covers the house, and Christ covers the Church, the male provides a covering for his descendents. The man who is submitted and obedient to God will see his seed blessed to the fourth generation.

The male also provides direction. It was the men who sat at the gates of the city throughout the Old Testament. They protected and directed the affairs of the community. They also provide a vision for the future. Joel prophesied, *"Your old men shall dream dreams, your young men shall see visions"* (Joel 2:28). In the Book of Acts, Peter reminds us that this still holds true today, *"In the last days, God says, I will pour out My Spirit on all people. Your sons and daughters will prophesy, your young men will see visions, your old men will dream dreams"* (Acts 2:17 NIV). Expect to dream and see visions of the future. Hold on to the promise hidden within your seed by faith, in prayer, and through obedience so your descendants will sit on the throne...to the fourth generation.

> *By Myself I have sworn, says the Lord...blessing I will bless you, and multiplying I will multiply your descendants as the stars of the heaven and as the sand which is on the seashore; and your descendants shall possess the gate of their enemies. In your seed all the nations of the earth shall be blessed, because you have obeyed My voice.* —GENESIS 22:16-18

Chapter 13

THE UTERUS OF A WOMAN

Whenever I held my newborn baby in my arms,
I used to think that what I said and did to him
could have an influence not only on him but on all
whom he met, not only for a day or a month or a
year, but for all eternity—a very challenging and
exciting thought for a mother. —ROSE KENNEDY

A mother carries human seed within her, where it germinates and grows until a new life is fully formed. A woman is designed to be God's divine incubator. She has an awesome role, privilege, and responsibility for protecting and nurturing the seed she carries and making sure that all of the possible things that could harm it are removed from the environment.

Once she conceives, her life is no longer her own. She doesn't eat the same things, do the same activities, or take the same risks.

The new life she carries within her takes precedence over all else. In a way, she is in a time of testing during which she must consecrate her entire existence to protecting the unborn child from all the forces that would come against it. Interestingly enough, the time required to complete this period is roughly nine months, or more precisely, forty weeks.

Both the number nine and the number forty are significant throughout the Bible. In the New Testament we read about the nine fruits of the Spirit (Galatians 5:22) and the nine gifts of the Spirit (1 Corinthians 12:8-10); and in the Old Testament we read about the nine judgments (Haggai 1:11). As nine is the last of the digits, it marks the end and therefore the conclusion of a matter. It is the number of fulfillment.

According to E. W. Bullinger, author of *Number in Scripture: Its Supernatural Design and Spiritual Significance*, "It is akin to the number six, six being the sum of its factors (3 x 3 = 9, and 3 + 3 = 6), and is thus significant of the end of man, and the summation of all man's works." Bullinger goes on to explain that "nine is, therefore, the number of finality or judgment…. It marks the completeness, the end and issue of all things as to man—the judgment of man and all his works."[40]

Equally significant to the duration of pregnancy are the forty weeks it represents. The number forty is associated with the fulfillment of promise as well as a phase of probation or trial. According to Todd Dennis and Richard Anthony, "The number forty is used by God to represent a period of testing or judgment (the length of time necessary to accomplish some major part of God's plan in His dealings with various portions of mankind)." They list as examples the "forty days of rain in the days of the flood…. The forty-day periods of fasting, testing, and communing with God faced by Moses and Jesus….

The forty years the Israelites spent in the wilderness were [all forms of] the judgments of God."[41]

E. W. Bullinger concurs:

> Forty has long been universally recognized as an important number, both on account of the frequency of its occurrence, and the uniformity of its association with a period of probation, trial, and chastisement. It is the product of 5 and 8, and points to the action of grace (5), leading to and ending in revival and renewal (8).[42]

Christ and the children of Israel were tested in the wilderness over a period of forty days and forty years, respectively. They were tested in three distinct areas. The three temptations of Christ give us insight into the tests put before the Israelites. In Exodus 20:20 Moses reassured the children of Israel with these words, *"Do not fear; God has come to test you, and that His fear may be before you, so that you may not sin."* If they could learn to honor God in these areas, to align their hearts with His will and His ways, they would be poised to fulfill their greatest potential and inherit all that God had prepared for them.

Jesus did just that on our behalf when He overcame every temptation of the devil during his forty-day trial in the desert. During that time, Christ was tempted to turn stone into bread—He was tempted to do for Himself what only God could do for Him. Likewise, the children of Israel were tempted by a lack of bread. But God demonstrated His ability to provide for them what they could not provide for themselves.

Second, Jesus was tested on whether He would take God at His Word or test Him. Jesus said, *"It is also written: 'Do not put the Lord your God to the test'"* (Matthew 4:7 NIV). The Israelites, on the other hand, tested God repeatedly. They constantly complained about their condition, needs, and leaders, and worse, when they finally arrived at their destination, they lacked faith to enter into it. Sound familiar? They tempted God through their lack of faith and perpetual disobedience and missed out on possessing God's promise.

The third area of testing was whether they would worship God, and only God, with their whole heart, which is the first commandment. *"Love the Lord your God with all your heart, with all your soul, with all your mind, and with all your strength"* (Mark 12:30). When Satan offered Jesus all the kingdoms of the world in exchange for His allegiance, Jesus responded, *"For it is written: 'Worship the Lord your God, and Him only you shall serve'"* (Matthew 4:10). The children of Israel didn't fare so well in this area either. While Moses was on the mountain receiving God's commandments, they were down below molding a golden calf to worship instead of God.

We can divide the earth's history from before the Flood to the present time into three "forty Jubilee" periods of testing as well. According to C. Gary Hullquist, author of *Sabbath Diagnosis*, there were forty Jubilees—or 1,960 years—that represented the "Flood Era" (during which people did not trust in God), and forty Jubilees that represented the "Jewish Era" (during which God was tempted time and time again), and forty Jubilees that represent the "Christian Era" (during which time people have been challenged to worship God in spirit and truth [John 4:23-24]).

A Jubilee cycle is seven times seven years, or forty-nine years. Forty represents the number of Jubilee cycles since Christ was crucified until the present time. The earth's probationary period is almost over. Paul reminds us in his letter to the Romans, *"For we know that the whole creation groans and labors with birth pangs together until now"* (Romans 8:22). Because even the earth has been pregnant with the divine promise of God: *"the creation itself also will be delivered from the bondage of corruption into the glorious liberty of the children of God"* (Romans 8:21).

It is common knowledge that a woman's pregnancy is divided into three trimesters, each characterized by a unique set of trials. The first trimester is when the mother may be tempted to question her ability to provide and choose to abort the baby out of fear. It is the most difficult because of the overwhelming uncertainly, sickness, and fatigue that accompany it. As with the Israelites and Jesus in the desert, this is a time during which she finds herself the most physically weak.

The second trimester is associated with the uneasiness of change and transformation. Although the energy and appetite return, this time requires a new level of trust in God's leading and what the future holds. It is easy to fall into periods of discontentment, restlessness, and impatience. Unlike the children of Israel, she must remain faithful and obedient, *"fitting every loose thought and emotion and impulse into the structure of life shaped by Christ"* (2 Corinthians 10:5 MSG).

The third trimester can be the most challenging due to the increasing pressure of the growing baby—the kicking, the backaches, the swelling; the difficulty in breathing, standing, and walking; doing even the most mundane tasks. But as the night is darkest before the dawn, so it is just before the baby is born. The task at hand may seem insurmountable, but she must not take her eyes off of the God of her salvation. It is important she continue *"looking unto Jesus, the author and finisher of our faith, who for the joy that was set before Him endured the cross, despising the shame, and has sat down at the right hand of the throne of God"* (Hebrews 12:2). The Israelites did not keep their focus on God but on the world in the form of a golden calf. Jesus, on the other hand, could not be persuaded to turn away from God for *"all the kingdoms of the world and their glory"* (Matthew 4:8).

Because women are carriers of the promise, because they are the incubators in which the seed of humanity germinates and grows, Satan works overtime to destroy them. In Genesis 3:15, God said, *"I will put enmity between you and the woman, and between your seed and her Seed."* There has always been supernatural vengeance against women throughout history. Even today around the globe we see women oppressed, abused, raped, and sold into slavery. There are more slaves in the world today than at any other time in history—and the majority of those slaves are young girls and women who are held in bondage to the sex trade. In some cultures, female castration, or genital mutilation, remains prevalent. These injustices are more demonic than cultural in nature and are aimed at a woman's reproductive organs because the enemy knows the power contained within the seed she carries—power to destroy his works in the earth.

In spite of all these factors, however, the strength of a woman is incredible. Women are resilient and have always affected the fate of nations. You will find that where women are disempowered and oppressed a weak and underdeveloped nation will be present, and where women are strengthened and empowered a strong and powerful nation will be there.

There is a saying that the hand that rocks the cradle rules the world. Every leader, every lawyer, every doctor, and every male has been birthed through a woman. If it is true that the hand that rocks the cradle rules the world, then if that hand is broken, you will have a broken world; if that hand is bruised, you'll have a bruised world; if that hand is hurt, you'll have a hurting world. So it is imperative for women to understand the significance of their role as mother. It is one of the greatest honors God has placed on anyone, because even as the Messiah was carried in the womb of a woman, so are women carrying the next generation of doctors and lawyers and movers and shakers.

By the God of your father who will help you, and by the Almighty who will bless you with blessings of heaven above, blessings of the deep that lies beneath, blessings of the breasts and of the womb. —GENESIS 49:25

Chapter 14

THE SPIRIT

But there is a spirit within people,
the breath of the Almighty within them,
that makes them intelligent. —JOB 32:8

I have heard it said that our physical body makes us world-conscious, our soul makes us self-conscious, and our spirit makes us God-conscious. God interacts with us through our spirit. He plants His Word, His will, and His promises within our heart. God revealed this through Isaiah when He said, *"My Spirit, Who is upon you…writes the law of God inwardly on the heart"* (Isaiah 59:21 AMP). He writes His Word on your heart by speaking to you through your spirit.

"All My words that I shall speak to you, receive in your heart and hear with your ears" (Ezekiel 3:10 AMP). He has given us ears to hear His voice, but we must be willing to listen. Again, God spoke through

Isaiah, *"Incline your ear, and come to Me. Hear, and your soul shall live"* (Isaiah 55:3). Through the prophet Jeremiah He instructed, *"Hear the word of the Lord…let your ear receive the word of His mouth"* (Jeremiah 9:20). And in Revelation He simply said, *"He who has an ear, let him hear"* (Revelation 13:9 NIV).

The ear is part of the reproductive organ of the sprit. Everything that you and I hear carries with it seedlings of possibility that are planted within the soil of our heart. What we hear from God is the kingdom being cultivated within our spirit being. *"To whom shall I speak…that they may hear? Indeed their ear is uncircumcised, and they cannot give heed"* (Jeremiah 6:10). We must be careful how we hear and what we allow to go into our spirit. We must be sensitive to the voice of God, rightly divide His Word to us personally, and sanctify it in our individual lives.

Your heart is fertile soil that will grow whatever is planted in it. Your spirit is like an inner garden that is sown with either the seeds of heaven, which are the purposes and promises found in the truth of God's Word, or the seeds of deception and destruction received from the messages of the enemy and the temporal world. One will bring a harvest of peace and righteousness, the other nothing but death and despair. What you put into your heart through what you hear and believe will ultimately determine the quality of your life. This is why we are told in Proverbs, *"Keep and guard your heart with all vigilance and above all that you guard, for out of it flow the springs of life"* (Proverbs 4:23 AMP). Springs of death can also flow from the heart as well.

God conveys His will and His kingdom into our hearts through our spiritual ears. Paul wrote to the Corinthians that *"the natural man does not receive the things of the Spirit of God…because they are spiritually discerned"* (1 Corinthians 2:14). The Spirit of God communicates with the spirit of man; however, because of circumstances or situations, we often may feel as if we really don't want to hear God anymore. We are overcome by disappointment and can get discouraged, allowing our spiritual self to disconnect with our life source. This is when a person becomes indifferent and hopeless and despairing of life because it is the spirit that sustains and upholds us. David cried out in the Psalms, *"Grant me a willing spirit, to sustain me"* (Psalm 51:12 NIV), and Solomon taught in Proverbs, *"A man's spirit sustains him"* (Proverbs 18:14 NIV).

God designed your being to be sustained by your spirit, and your spirit to be sustained by your hope in Him. Look what happened to the nation of Israel when they lost hope in God: *"We have become old, dry bones—all hope is gone"* (Ezekiel 37:11 NLT). And Proverbs tells us, *"Hope deferred makes the heart sick"* (Proverbs 13:12). Hope is a powerful force. It is an anchor and a lifeline. The writer of Hebrews put it this way: *"This hope is a strong and trustworthy anchor for our souls. It leads us through the curtain into God's inner sanctuary"* (Hebrews 6:19 NLT). The Message gives this interpretation for the same verse: *"It's an unbreakable spiritual lifeline, reaching past all appearances right to the very presence of God."* And John added that *"everyone who has this hope in Him purifies himself, just as He is pure"* (1 John 3:3).

We have this hope because *"He has planted eternity in the human heart"* (Ecclesiastes 3:11 NLT). In other words, His eternal purpose for our lives and even for nations—everything in the world—is hidden in our heart. This hope protects and purifies because it brings with it a sense of expectation and purpose.

As a seed is hidden in the womb of a woman and is germinated and incubated there, our spirit holds the developing seeds of our destiny. Have you ever been at a point in your life when you just felt like giving up, where you were so tired and weak you felt you couldn't continue exerting yourself? Yet somehow, at some point, you were able to push past that feeling—something on the inside pushed you past the discomfort, past the point of despair or discouragement, and past the pain of stretching and expanding your abilities.

As a mother pushes to give birth, ready to give up at any moment from sheer exhaustion, an irresistible force compels her to keep pushing. We are not always in tune with what God is doing in and through us as He is birthing His purpose for our lives. Nevertheless, a force greater than ourselves prompts us to press through that threshold, that invisible barrier, and then we are able to see the new life that has come forth from our trial.

This is what makes inventors, scientists, artists, authors, activists, entrepreneurs, educators, and heroes of every kind so profound. Where an ordinary person would have given up, they were able to tap into the divine assignment hidden in their heart. They had the drive and the fire on the inside of them that they could not shake off. Jeremiah said, *"His word was in my heart like a burning fire shut up in my bones; I was weary of holding it back, and I could not"* (Jeremiah 20:9). Jeremiah determined to never preach again, yet he could not keep from delivering the prophecy he was created to deliver. This is something God hides deep within your spirit. It is time sensitive and has a statute of limitations for remaining hidden. When it is time for it to be expressed is when the urge to push comes. There is no holding it back when the time for delivery is due.

Your assignment and purpose are hidden in your spirit. This hope—God's eternal purpose—is what God hides in you and will reveal through you in due time. Jesus said, *"There is nothing hidden which will not be revealed"* (Mark 4:22). Guard your heart and listen for God's voice. Be faithful with what He gives you to do and say each and every day. Practice bringing what God shows you in the inner sanctum of your heart to the surface, bringing what He whispers to you in the darkness into broad daylight. For Jesus said, *"Whatever I tell you in the dark, speak in the light; and what you hear in the ear, preach on the housetops"* (Matthew 10:27).

> *Who among you will give ear to this? Who will listen and hear for the time to come?* —ISAIAH 42:23

> *He who believes in Me, as the Scripture has said, out of his heart will flow rivers of living water.* —JOHN 7:38

Chapter 15

THE MIND

What we are today comes from our thoughts of yesterday,
and our present thoughts build our life of tomorrow: Our
life is the creation of our mind. —GAUTAMA SIDDHARTA

Thoughts are not only produced by a series of neurological processes, but by what is the mystery of the spirit of the mind. When God created man, He created him as a thinking being—in His image and likeness. God created humans with the ability to think, imagine, and create. Paul asked the Corinthians, *"Who has known the mind of the Lord that he may instruct Him?"* (1 Corinthians 2:16). In the same verse he also gave the answer, *"But we have the mind of Christ."* You and I have been given the mind of God in Christ—the great womb of all creation. Like God's mind, our mind has been endued with divine creative power. The power of our thoughts, intentions, and words can manifest new realities, create something from nothing, and they can even alter the physical universe.

Dr. William Tiller, author of *Conscious Acts of Creation: The Emergence of a New Physics*, has set out to scientifically prove that mind affects matter. "We humans are much more than we think we are and Psychoenergetic Science continues to expand the proof of it,"[44] he writes. His experiments to demonstrate the effect of mind over matter began by imprinting electrical devices with a specific intention. He started by instructing four experienced meditation practitioners to focus their minds on the device with the intention to change the pH of water. The device was wrapped in aluminum and sent by overnight shipping to a laboratory two thousand miles away. When a jar of water was placed in the vicinity of the electrical device, the water's pH changed by as much as one and a half full units, which is a very large amount.

It was when the same experiment was repeated over and over that the really significant effects began to show. Tiller has discovered and scientifically proven that when intent is repeated in the same space, eventually it becomes permanent. And when *that* happens, the laws of physics in that space no longer operate as they did before. When they kept running the same experiment over and over again, Tiller says, the laboratory began to become "conditioned" so that the same result would happen more strongly or more quickly. And eventually, it would happen even after the device was no longer in the room.

"In one of the spaces that we have used," Tiller says, "the alteration in the space of the room has remained stable for well over a year, and it's still going strong."[45] In physical terms, what does this mean? What has actually happened to the "space" of the laboratory room? Tiller explains:

The experimental data we gather seems to indicate that it raises what is called the "physics gauge symmetry" of the room. In a "normal space," the magnetic force is proportional to the gradient of the square of the magnetic field. In this "conditioned space," we've raised the gauge symmetry from the U{1} Gauge to something approximating what is called the SU{2} Gauge. Very big effects.... That says that we are producing domains of order in the vacuum![46]

What this basically means is that a law of physics has been changed in this space. Tiller has shown that the order thus created in the vacuum is affected by human intent, proving that the power of the vacuum can actually be harnessed through our consciousness.[47]

Quantum mechanics and relativity theory are the two prime theoretical constructs of modern physics, and for quantum mechanics and relativity theory to be internally self-consistent, their calculations require that the vacuum must contain an energy density 1094 grams per cubic centimeter.[48]

In other words, if you multiply the volume of a single hydrogen atom by the average mass density of the cosmos, you will discover that within the amount of vacuum contained in this hydrogen atom there is, according to this calculation, "almost a trillion times as much energy as in all of the stars and all of the planets out to a radius of 20 billion light years!"[49] He continues:

If human consciousness can interact with that even a little bit, it can change things in matter. Because the ground state energies of all particles have that energy level due to their interaction with this stuff of the vacuum. So if you can shift that stuff of the vacuum, change its degree of order or coherence even a little bit, you can change the ground state energies of particles, atoms, molecules, and chemical equations.[50]

Our future, Dr. Tiller is telling us, lies in harnessing the energies that lie hidden in the spaces between the particles, atoms, molecules, planets, stars, and galaxies of the physical universe. "Matter as we know it," Tiller concludes poetically, "is hardly a fragrance of a whisper."[51]

Our minds truly do act as the wombs of creation. What we see as the inalterable physical universe is but a ripple in God's imagination echoing His intentions. God said, *"Let Us [Father, Son, and Holy Spirit] make mankind in Our image, after Our likeness, and let them have complete authority"* (Genesis 1:26 AMP). Not only do we have God's mind, but we are also His holy temple (1 Corinthians 6:19).

I found it interesting when I studied the etymological history of the word *womb*. The ancient Sanskrit word for "temple" or "sanctuary" was the same word that was used for "womb," carrying the connotation of a "gateway" or "portal." The oldest oracle in Greece was named Delphi, derived from the word *delphos,* or "womb." This is how the brilliant Swiss painter Paul Klee described the meaning of the word: "From which all functions derive their life....In the womb of nature, in the primal ground of creation, where the secret key to all things lies hidden."[52]

Consider for a moment the possibility that the secret key to all things lies hidden in your mind—the gateway or portal, the sanctuary or birthing place of all things. That thought is pregnant with possibilities.

> *So God created man in His own image, in the image and likeness of God He created him.* —GENESIS 1:27 AMP

Ah! From the soul itself must issue forth
A light, a glory, a fair luminous cloud
Enveloping the Earth.
And from the soul itself must there be sent
A sweet and potent voice, of its own birth
Of all sweet sounds the life and element!
—SAMUEL TAYLOR COLERIDGE

Chapter 16

THE BODY

*Our own physical body possesses a wisdom, which
we who inhabit the body lack. We give it orders
which make no sense.* —HENRY MILLER

*Emotion always has its roots in the unconscious
and manifests itself in the body.* —IRENE
CLAREMONT DE CASTILLEJO

Dr. Deepak Chopra is a traditionally trained medical doctor as well as an expert in alternative forms of treatment and psychoneuroimmunology. He is the author of *Quantum Healing, Perfect Health* and *Ageless Body, Timeless Mind*, both of which teach the underlying essentials of achieving vibrant health and longevity. In these two books, he introduces readers to the concept that the human body is an exquisite biochemical, self-sustaining mechanism with infinite regenerative power.

The human body can be compared to a computer, which stores vast amounts of information on its hard drive. The key to health then is the ability to read, interpret, and manage the data being stored while responding to the prompts and signals our bodies give, indicating the need for adjustments. Our bodies are nothing but a system of telecommunication networks that simultaneously control the smallest to the biggest processes—from the reactions of a cell to the contractions of major muscle groups. If we can get in touch with these processes, we can undoubtedly eliminate ninety percent of our biological or biochemical or bioelectrical malfunctions, conditions, sicknesses, and diseases!

Our bodies are the vehicles that will take us into our future and destiny. If we do not treat them as the valuable treasures they are, we will find that we will be increasingly less productive and unsuccessful in accomplishing our dreams and visions. On the other hand, by making some fairly simple adjustments to the way we maintain our bodies, we can radically improve our health and productivity, add longevity, and increase the overall quality of our lives.

The human body is in a constant state of change that maintains a level equilibrium needed for balanced function. In addition, the body completely regenerates itself every year. Our bodies are magnificent dynamic systems, constantly changing, and are held together and informed by a biochemical framework like the mainframe of a computer.

Within the atomic fiber of our being resides a tenacious cellular memory. It is as powerful as the subconscious memories of our mind that cause us to experience the same life patterns over and over, regardless of our intentions to change. Our bodies, much like our minds, seem to default to an automated pilot unless we purposefully take the controls and override the navigational system. The body will continue regenerating itself with the same cellular configurations of disorders and ailments unless we reprogram its configuration.

The most basic functions of the body work on a molecular level. Many molecules make up cells which themselves are grouped to form tissues. Various tissues are arranged in a particular fashion; these units are what comprise organs. The body's systems are made up of groups of organs that communicate through the bloodstream in order to continually monitor and adjust the body's mass network of functions. We are dealing with the "issues of the tissues" when we talk about improving health and increasing longevity. The first step to maximizing your body's capacity to move through life as a powerful vehicle, one that is built like an armored truck but drives like a luxury sports car, is to understand that prevention and correction are dealt with on the most basic molecular level.

There are many ways to reprogram your body, some with more lasting effects than others. You can experience long-term weight loss by increasing your body's metabolism. All you have to do is increase your daily exercise and eat six small, protein-packed meals every day. Or you can quickly drop water weight in just a matter of days by going on various types of fasts. However, as soon as you stop fasting, you will put all the weight, plus some, back on! For lasting change, you need to work at the cellular level, where you actually burn energy or metabolize calories. Withholding food causes your metabolism to slow down, and that's why diets and fasts don't work for long-term weight loss.

You have to get at the root of the issue—into the tissue of the issue. Just as quick-fix diets don't work, neither do medications that deal only with the symptoms and not the root causes of illness. If you do not adjust your lifestyle, your belief systems, and your emotional state, which are the root causes of eighty percent of sickness and disease, medications will provide only temporary relief and, in most cases, cause problems in other areas. It's a vicious cycle of side effects and complications requiring more medications that create more imbalances and worse complications than the original issue.

Antibiotics, for example, are given for bacterial illnesses and infections (that, consequently, only take hold when the immune system is compromised due to our own negligence). Most illness can be flushed out of the body within seven to ten days with or without medication. After taking a series of antibiotics, however, you are vulnerable to yeast infections because the antibiotic will have killed all of the good bacteria in your system along with the bad. Yeast infections take weeks, and sometimes even months, to eradicate. And not only can yeast infections lead to bladder infections, but medications prescribed for these types of infections commonly cause rashes and other abnormalities. The cycle just never ends.

Pain or discomfort is actually more of an ally than an enemy. Pain is simply your body's way of signaling the need for adjustment. Instead of immediately trying to get rid of the pain by masking it, learn to embrace it and explore the root cause. Bodily discomfort can be compared to spiritual or emotional discomfort. When something doesn't feel right, like when you don't have a peace about something or sometimes you feel guilty or ashamed, it can be an indicator that something is amiss. Perhaps you need to reevaluate some things, make some adjustments, apologize, forgive, or repent.

Trust your spirit *and* your body. Both were given to you by God—you are created in the image and likeness of Him. Listen to the signals and heed the warning signs. Don't be too quick to mask what your body is trying to tell you; give it some credit for knowing how to take care of itself and a chance to work on your behalf. The mind of your body has the best interests of your body in mind. Let it think for itself. Don't be too quick to fall for the world's interpretations and methods when it comes to your health.

You've heard the old saying, "Feed a cold; starve a fever." That doesn't make much sense when you look at how the body actually works. When you are sick, your body needs to detoxify on a number of levels. For example, rather than eating when you have a cold, you should be fasting so that the body can locate the exact biochemical elixir from its exquisite pharmacy and produce a better quality healing compound, made in its very own lab, and then administer the correct dose without side effects (and so much cheaper). The body will use the energies you would normally use to digest food to begin the process of healing.

I am not a medical doctor nor am I a psychiatrist. What I am is a psychotherapeutic holistic consultant. I am not attempting to give diagnostic evaluations but physiological observations with suggestions of probable root emotional causes with affirmations and antidotes, which you can use as a tool to reverse sickness and disease. And hopefully by this time next year you will have reprogrammed your body at a cellular level for a totally new and improved you. Maya Angelou said, "Do the best you can until you know better. Then when you know better, do better."

Here are some small investments you can make for massive health returns:

ATTITUDE	• Maintain an attitude of gratitude. • Don't sweat the small stuff—or the stuff that really isn't significant to your goals, purpose, and destiny—such as insignificant people, insignificant things, insignificant circumstances. • Put your uniqueness on display. • Choose your emotional state. • Remember emotions follow motion. • De-stress your life. • Listen to uplifting music. • Watch an inspirational movie.
NUTRITION	• Eat so that you create an environment within your body where it will be hard for disease to thrive. • East live/living food. Remember, you really are what you eat. • Supplement live food with vitamins and herbs. (Remember, if you eat dead food you will be supplementing death.) • Eat whole, authentic, real food. Avoid GMOs. • Eat to live; don't live to eat (but do mindfully enjoy every mouthful).
EXERCISE	Remember your psychology follows your physiology. • Get outside, get your daily dose of vitamin D, and absorb the natural healing power of sunshine. • Get out of your office. Get out of your house. • Get out and walk fifteen to thirty minutes every day. • Get moving! Bike, skate, dance, jog, run, do aerobics, play tennis, lift weights, just move it!
WATER	• Drink *at least* eight glasses of water per day. • Drink reverse osmosis purified water. • Use a water purifier if you drink tap water, and be sure to drink out of a glass, ceramic, or stainless steel container if you purchase water.
SPIRITUAL & EMOTIONAL ENRICHMENT	• Spend time with God. • Worship. • Pray. • Meditate. • Nurture your soul. • Spend time with others. • Cultivate loving, supportive, mutually beneficial relationships. • Get rid of toxic relationships.

TIME MANAGEMENT	• Manage time according to your purpose, vision, responsibilities, and assignment. • Remember, someone else's emergency does not constitute an emergency for you. • Practice creating strong time (and relationship) boundaries. • Remember that you control your time; time and other people should not control you
AIR	Oxygenate your life: • Take cleansing breaths, forcing out the stale air and filling your lungs with fresh air. • Take long walks outside, by the ocean, in the mountains, through the woods. • Breath deeply. • Buy an ionizer for the house.

REST AND RELAXATION	• Even God took a sabbath—take a day to rest.
	• To be more productive take:
	    Half a morning plus half an afternoon off weekly
	    One weekend per month
	    Five days per quarter
	    Three weeks per year
	    And don't feel guilty about it!

TIME FOR SELF	• Get alone and enjoy some "me moments."
	• Detoxify your mind, soul, and body regularly.
	• Read.
	• Write in a journal.
	• Go for a walk.
	• Learn something new.
	• Take up a new hobby.
	• Laugh at yourself.
	• Laugh at your mistakes.
	• Laugh at nothing.
	• Play.
	• Discover:
	    Who you really are
	    What you really want
	    What you really like
	    What makes you happy
	    Where you are going
	• Sing your happy song out loud.
	• Watch an inspirational movie.

Do all of this and I guarantee that you will be a totally new you in no time at all.

*Although the whole man partakes of this grace,
it is first and most appropriately in the soul and
later progresses to the body, inasmuch as the body
of the man is capable of the same obedience to the
will of God as the soul.* —WILLIAM AMES

*Take care of your body. It's the only place
you have to live.* —JIM ROHN

*Don't you realize that your body is the temple of
the Holy Spirit, who lives in you and was given to
you by God? You do not belong to yourself, for God
bought you with a high price. So you must honor God
with your body.* —1 CORINTHIANS 6:19-29 NLT

*So there is a special rest still waiting for the people
of God. For all who have entered into God's rest
have rested from their labors, just as God did after
creating the world. So let us do our best to enter
that rest. But if we disobey God, as the people of
Israel did, we will fall.* —HEBREWS 4:9-10 NLT

Wombs of Consciousness

GIVING BIRTH TO HOW WE THINK

Chapter 17

THOUGHT

Thoughts give birth to a creative force that is neither elemental nor sidereal. Thoughts create a new heaven, a new firmament, a new source of energy, from which new arts flow. When a man undertakes to create something, he establishes a new heaven, as it were, and from it the work that he desires to create flows into him. For such is the immensity of man that he is greater than heaven and earth. —Philipus Aureolus Paracelsus, German (Swiss-born) alchemist and physician (1493–1541)

The significant problems we have cannot be solved at the same level of thinking with which we created them. —Albert Einstein

You are either the captive or the captain of your thoughts. —Denis Waitley

If the mind can be likened to the soil of a garden, then thoughts would be the seeds we plant in that soil. Scientists have found that the average person thinks about 50,000 thoughts a day—that's a lot of seed! How much of what you are sowing is fruit-bearing and how much is more like thistle? The quality of the harvest of your life is determined by the quality and quantity of the seed you sow or by the thoughts you cultivate. A thought, like a seed, is a container of life and potential that must be nurtured—fed, watered, protected, and harvested.

There are thoughts that hold the key to your future and thoughts that can trip you up and choke the life force hidden within the amazing realm of cognition. Refuse to allow one weed to take over your seed of greatness, success, prosperity, wealth, righteousness, holiness, influence, affluence, favor, or peace. Your thoughts determine who you are, what you do, what you acquire, where you live, whom you love, who you will become, and what you will accomplish. You will never have more, go further, or accomplish greater things than what you can comprehend. Your feet will never take you where your mind has never been. Your background, education, or IQ cannot prohibit you from thinking. Never lose the power to think for yourself.

You must create a thinking environment, practice thinking for yourself, and then learn to think outside of the box. Your thoughts are powerful and you have a God-given capacity to think potent thoughts. Grab hold of the concept of "possibility thinking." If you can't think it, then it won't be possible for you. On the other hand, if you can think big, amazing thoughts, you will experience a big, amazing life. In the words of writer William Arthur Ward, "Nothing limits achievement like small thinking."

Your thoughts determine your destiny. I've heard it said, "Your destiny determines your legacy, and when you die your legacy determines your history." Think about your future, what you truly want to accomplish in life, and what steps you need to take to reach your goal.

That's exactly what a pharmacist named Dr. John Stith Pemberton did when he took a jug of his cough syrup to a local drug store where carbonated water was added to produce what we now know as Coca-Cola. It was then bottled and marketed around the world. Today there is hardly a person on the planet who is not familiar with the name. Pemberton was able to think outside the box and expand the field of possibility.

Thought is defined as a "mental picture of something such as a future or possible event... an expectation or hope that something will happen."[53] I found this next great definition online; pay special attention to what I emphasized:

> Thought and thinking are mental forms and processes, respectively ("thought" is both). Thinking allows beings to *model the world* and to deal with it effectively according to their objectives, plans, ends, and desires.... Thinking involves the mental manipulation of information, as when we form concepts, engage in problem solving, reason, and make decisions.[54]

Thought allows you to model the world according to your objectives and desires. The power tool of your thoughts is the most important tool you have when it comes to framing your world; it is also the most effective weapon you have against the enemy. Learn to focus your thoughts—harness and use them for maximum results. The quality of your life is determined by the quality of your thoughts. You can begin today developing powerful thought habits that will turbo-charge your journey to destiny. Make the thought habits I've listed below a daily practice.

THINK CREATIVELY

The secret to creativity begins with understanding how to mind your success. Create an atmosphere for creativity by uncluttering your environment. Orderly surroundings will help you order your thoughts. Minding your success also means practicing being heavenly-minded. When you think heaven's thoughts, you are aligning your thoughts with God's thoughts.

Creator God created us in His image and after His likeness. God created the heavens, the earth, and everything in between. If you and I are created in His image, then we are creators too. Tap into the creative mind of God to see what others don't make the effort to see and hear what others are not able to hear because they don't operate on your heavenly frequency. When you do this, you will get a hold of what others have not yet been able to. That's all creativity is—yielding to the mind of God, allowing God's creative Spirit to flow through you.

Open wide the spiritual channel of your mind so that divine creative thoughts begin to flow. Ask God to enlarge your capacity to think; ask the Holy Spirit to take the limits off your imagination. Knowing you are the creator of your reality, pray the Lord would give you insight, ideas, and inspiration you've never had before; open your mind to all the possibilities available to you in Christ. In the words of wealth creator Robert Allen, "All that a man achieves and all that he fails to achieve is the direct result of his own thoughts."

THINK STRATEGICALLY

Plan your work and work your plan. Clearly define your goals and review your objectives daily. What are you doing today that will bring you closer to fulfilling your goals? Develop timelines.

Goals are time-bound—SMART goals are Specific, Measurable, Attainable, Results-oriented, and Time sensitive. SMART goals provide focus and define exactly what the "future state" looks like and how it will be measured. Remember that a goal without a deadline is only a dream.

THINK GENERATIONALLY

Ask yourself what kind of legacy you want to leave for the next generation? Where do you want to be in twenty or forty years from now? Get a vision for why you are here and what you are called to do that will leave a lasting impact. How will your life influence the next generation? How will you be remembered? James Allen, the author of the revolutionary book *As A Man Thinketh*, wrote, "You are today where your thoughts have brought you; you will be tomorrow where your thoughts take you."

THINK SEEDFULLY

Human begins are procreators. We were created to procreate; and we are pros at creating! Learn to think entrepreneurially, fruitfully, and exponentially. Be an active participant in creating and expanding life.

LEARN TO FOCUS YOUR THOUGHTS

Whatever you focus on has the power to change your future. Do not focus on things, people, or circumstances you do not expect to see in your future. Your focus will either expose your faith or confirm your fear. Mastering the art of concentration will give you power over your life. Without focus your aspirations will turn into desperation, desperation will turn into deprivation, deprivation into depression, and depression into disillusion.

THINK DIVERGENTLY

Take a risk. The biggest risk in life is not to have taken any risks at all. It's not important that you know how you're going to do it, just know that you *will* do it. When that happens, the whole universe conspires with heaven to make certain you do.

THINK SUCCESSFULLY

Think in the present. Think positively. Think as if you are already doing what you've purposed in your heart to do. See the thing that you want as already yours. Accomplish it in your mind. Receive it. Take possession of it in your thoughts. Condition your mind to embrace and live in this new reality as if it were already here.

Continually ask yourself these four questions:

- Why?

- Why not?

- Why not me?

- Why not now?

Practice IT— "Intentional Thinking": Live on purpose. Imagination + Intention + Action = Manifestation.

THINK SCRIPTURALLY

Practice *"taking every thought captive to the obedience of Christ"* (2 Corinthians 10:5 NASB). And then *"be transformed by the renewing of your mind"* (Romans 12:2). How do you renew your mind? You practice filling it with God-ordained thoughts as described in Philippians 4:8: *"Fix your thoughts on what is true, and honorable, and right, and pure, and lovely, and admirable. Think about things that are excellent and worthy of praise"* (NLT).

Take personal responsibility for your thoughts, because you are the product of your thoughts. You are what you think. The state of your life is the direct product of every thought you have allowed to access your mind. Even if you don't think much of anything, that's what you are producing. People who don't put any thought into their future will find they have nothing when they get there. But people who think about their future engineer it beforehand so that when it arrives it has shape and substance. See yourself where you want to be next year, in five years, in ten, and in twenty-five years.

> *For as he thinks within himself, so he*
> *is.* —**PROVERBS 23:7** NASB

Chapter 18

INTENTION

Once you make a decision, the universe conspires to
make it happen. —RALPH WALDO EMERSON

As I sat to write this chapter, I pondered the meaning of the word *intention* from a philosophical perspective. I asked myself whether I had ever intended to do some specific thing and experienced a positive outcome as a result, and conversely, how many positive outcomes I have experienced as the result of no specific intention. All of a sudden, this one word took on a profound meaning for me. I could see the correlation between the strength of my intention and the force of my influence.

In my research since then, I have discovered that the Latin *in-ten-dere* means to "stretch out." Psychologist and philosopher Elliot Jacques phrased it like this: "We have the vivid picture of the 'mind' as an outreaching, stretching, seeking, intention-riddled agency, seeking purposefully what it needs."[55]

There are many books and articles written about the act and consequences of intention. This is my theory in a nutshell: When a person actively intends to do something, it is like turning the volume knob up on success while muting failure. Your intention turns up the volume on positive expectations because it turns down doubt and fear; it mutes that part of the limbic system responsible for negative and destructive thoughts and emotions.

The limbic system is the part of your brain that supports the functioning of emotions, memories, attitudes, and senses—it is primarily located in sub-cortex. Intention, on the other hand, has a higher and more potent influence on the brain and emanates from the powerful prefrontal cortex, or "judgment center." According to the *American Heritage Dictionary*, an *intention* is "an aim that guides action." It is the guiding compass that leads you to Success Avenue, which runs adjacent to Accomplishment Boulevard. Intentions are the precursors to achievement and success.

In the 1940s Ronald Reagan was a major box office draw in Hollywood and had already appeared in more than two dozen movies. During the late '50s and early '60s, he became even more famous when he hosted the number one rated show on television, *General Electric Theater*. He also served as a president of the Screen Actors Guild for seven years. By 1964 Reagan was looking for a new challenge and auditioned for the starring role in an upcoming movie, *The Best Man*. He was not selected for the role because, according to an executive at United Artists, "Reagan doesn't have that presidential look." The role went instead to Henry Fonda.

Reagan decided that if he could not play the part of a great political leader in film, he would assume that role in real life as Governor of California. He went on to become the 40th President of the United States of America. He is quoted as saying, "Every new day begins with possibilities. It is up to us to fill it with the things that move us toward progress and peace."[56] One of those things, I believe, is intention.

Dr. Wayne Dyer, in his book *The Power of Intention,* sees intention as an energy created by the subconscious mind that brings thought from the causal realm into physical form. He believes that intention fosters creativity, which is a force that helps expand your awareness of what is possible in your life. Positive intentions can reframe your world, reengineer your life, and redesign your future. Intentions are powerful because they do not carry preconceived notions of how a thing can be accomplished, but only the raw belief that a thing *can* be accomplished. Intention is powerful because it sees only the opportunity unencumbered by obstacles. It opens the mind to the realm of pure potentiality and allows thoughts to flow in a limitless world of creativity. Intention is giving yourself permission to live the life of your dreams.

It is important to develop what I call "Intentional Thinking." I have nicknamed this concept "IT" and practice it intentionally every day. Without IT in the mix, you won't achieve all that you are capable of or live the life of your dreams. Coupled with imagination and action, you have the formula for unlimited success. Simply put, "Imagination + Intention + Action = Manifestation." If you don't practice IT on a regular basis, you will find that no matter how big you dream or how hard you work, you will never go far. You will find you are only gunning your engine but not going anywhere.

Practice living on purpose and see where it takes you. Every day when you awake, begin the day by setting your intention. Start each day by practicing intentional thinking. Be intentional about your success.

For which of you, intending to build a tower, does not sit down first and count the cost, whether he has enough to finish it—lest, after he has laid the foundation, and is not able to finish, all who see it begin to mock him. —LUKE 14:28-29

Chapter 19

IMAGINATION

Dreams are the seedlings of realities. —JAMES ALLEN

If the mind can be likened to a field and a thought to a seed, then it is the imagination that keeps it all irrigated. Human cognition is based on imagination—a phenomena unique to the human species, allowing us to live in the world of tomorrow today. Imagination is the ability to form a mental image of something that is not perceived through the senses. It is the ability of the mind to build mental scenes, objects, or events that do not exist, are not present, or have not already happened. Imagination makes it possible to experience a whole world inside the mind. It gives human beings the ability to look at any situation from a different point of view, enabling a person to mentally explore the plausible past, the potential present, and the possible future.

A developed and strong imagination is a great tool for re-creating and remodeling your world and life; it is a tremendous gift with amazing implications. Imagination fuels the creativity necessary for inventing, designing, engineering, illustrating, composing, and even researching scientific theory. The creative power of imagination has a vital role in achieving success in any field.

Visualizing an object or a situation and repeating this mental image often attracts the object or situation into our lives. While our imaginations open new and fascinating opportunities, we must be careful what we allow ourselves to imagine. We have to harness our imagination, rein in the silly string of our thoughts to stay positive about our desires. Otherwise we may create and attract into our lives events, situations, and people we don't really want. This is actually what most of us do because we don't use the power of imagination correctly. If we do not recognize the power of our imagination and we allow it to run wild, our life experiences may not reflect our truest desires.

The lack of understanding of the power of imagination is largely responsible for the suffering, difficulties, failures, and unhappiness people experience in the world. For some reason, most people are inclined to think negatively. They do not expect success. They expect the worst, and when they fail they believe that fate is against them. When this attitude is changed, when a person's imagination and expectations change, then life will improve accordingly.

I read a profound and dramatic story of an Air Force colonel who was a prisoner of war held in a Vietnamese prison for seven mentally and emotionally exhausting years. Every day this man played a full game of golf in his imagination. Exactly one week after he was released from his ordeal, he entered the Greater New Orleans Open and shot a seventy-six, which is an amazing score for a man who hadn't picked up a club in all of those years. This story illustrates the basic principle of harnessing your imagination—in other words, acting as if that which you perceive is real and already accomplished. I am not talking about pretending here, but about living and acting as if what you desire has already occurred. The problem with most people is that they dwell on what they don't have at the expense of what they can have.

You are not required to accept your life as it is. You do not have to accept your present circumstances but can live the life of your most daring dreams. In one of my favorite books of the Bible, Jesus tells a man who had been lame for thirty-eight years to take up his bed and walk (John 5). To me his bed represented the thirty-eight years he went to sleep and dreamed of a better life. You do not have to be limited to only dreams of a better life, but you can take up your bed and walk them out here and now.

Everything in the universe, every progress of humanity, every scientific advancement evolved from someone's imagination. The Book of Genesis shares many stories of the incredible power of imagination. In Genesis 13 we read of Abraham receiving the following instruction from the Lord:

> Lift your eyes now and look from the place where you are—northward, southward, eastward, and westward; for all the land which you see I give to you and your descendants forever.... Arise, walk in the land through its length and its width, for I give it to you (Genesis 13:14-17).

Abraham did not physically walk through its length and its width. He used his imagination to do so. God was simply saying he must have a clear vision of his future in order for it to come to pass. Abraham had to take responsibility in order to energize and materialize it with the power of his own imagination.

Where you find yourself ten years from now will be the direct result of your imagination. Visualize exactly where you want to be. Focus on what you want, not on what you don't want. Imagine the best *you* living your best life, doing your best work for God. You can do the same thing with your finances, your relationships, your marriage, or your business. Your imagination will influence every area of your life, for better or for worse. Don't imagine how terribly you could fail; dare to imagine how much you can achieve. In Genesis 11:6 God remarked, *"Nothing will be restrained from them, which they have imagined to do"* (KJV).

You must dare to imagine a fabulous future, one in which all your dreams come true. Charge your imagination with emotions and fuel it with action. Put yourself where you see yourself. Dare to go there. Arnold Schwarzenegger, five-time Mr. Universe and four-time Mr. Olympia, stated, "I visualized myself being there already, having achieved the goals already. It's mind over matter."[57]

As an exercise, think of anything about your life you would like to change or enhance. Sit back, relax, close your eyes, and fantasize about what you would really like to occur. Don't put any limitations on it and don't shroud it with doubt. Remember, there is no one who is going to judge this fantasy and no one who is going to prevent it from happening. Only you have the power to inhibit its realization. If it is healing in your body, then imagine yourself as you felt during your healthiest hour. Embrace that awareness and relive it as a real occurrence in the now. Henry David Thoreau said, "The world is but a canvas to the imagination."

In his book, *Stumbling on Happiness*, Daniel Gilbert wrote:

To see is to experience the world as it is, to remember is to experience the world as it was, but to imagine, ah, to imagine is to experience the world as it isn't and has never been, but as it might be. The greatest achievement of the human brain is its ability to imagine objects and episodes that do not exist in the realm of the real, and it is this ability that allows us to think about the future. As one philosopher noted, the human brain is an "anticipation machine," and "making future" is the most important function.[58]

The power of using visualization to create and invent can be demonstrated by the early experiences of Nikola Tesla. At a young age, Tesla began training his powers of imagination through actively visualizing his ideas. In his autobiography, *My Inventions*, Tesla wrote, "I observed to my delight that I could visualize with the greatest facility. I needed no models, drawings, or experiments. I could picture them all as real in my mind."[59] He further explained:

I gave myself up entirely to the intense enjoyment of picturing machines and devising new forms. It was a mental state of happiness about as complete as I have ever known in life. Ideas came in an uninterrupted stream and the only difficulty I had was to hold them fast.[60]

Tesla was a prolific and unparalleled genius without whom we might not have the advancements in radio, auto ignition, transmission, telephone, or television that we have today.

Never underestimate the power of your imagination. In the famous words of the legendary Napoleon Hill, "Whatever the mind of man can conceive, and believe, it can achieve."

Strip yourselves of your former nature [put off and discard your old unrenewed self] which characterized your previous manner of life and becomes corrupt through lusts and desires that spring from delusion; and be constantly renewed in the spirit of your mind [having a fresh mental and spiritual attitude], and put on the new nature (the regenerate self) created in God's image, [Godlike] in true righteousness and holiness. —EPHESIANS 4:22-24 AMP

Chapter 20

ATTITUDES

I discovered I always have choices and sometimes it's
only a choice of attitude. —JUDITH M. KNOWLTON

There once was a woman who, after taking chemotherapy, woke up one morning, looked in the mirror, and noticed she had only four strands of hair left. She said, "I know what I will do; I will wear two pig tails." She did and had a fantastic day. The next morning she awakened to find only three hairs on her head. "Well," she said, "I think I'll braid my hair today!" So she did and she had another wonderful day. The next day she woke up, looked in the mirror, and saw that she had only two hairs on her head. "Hmm," she said, "I think I'll part my hair down the middle today." So she did and she had a grand day.

The next day she woke up, looked in the mirror, and noticed that she had only one hair on her head. "Well," she said, "today I'm going to wear my hair in a pony tail." So she did and she had a fun, fun day. The next day she woke up, just grateful to be alive, looked in the mirror and noticed that there wasn't a single hair on her head. "Hooray!" she exclaimed. "I don't have to fix my hair today!" Well, the chemotherapy was successful, and it was only a year later that she looked into the same mirror at a full head of hair and thought, "It looks like I am going to have another beautiful day!"

Her story encouraged me as I wrote this chapter and reminded me that my happiness, joy, and peace are incubated and cultivated by my own attitude. Seldom considered, attitude does more to influence every area of our life than any other single thing. Attitude determines our altitude. It dictates how successful and, ultimately, how happy we will be. It not only controls how we handle life's challenges, but it also determines how we feel when we get up in the morning and the state of our being before we go to bed at night. It controls what we eat and drink, which ultimately determines the state of our health. And attitude, without a doubt, controls the health of our relationships.

Attitude controls the gate of creativity in your mind, the thoughts that you allow your mind to entertain, and the ideas that are cultivated resulting in products and services you can eventually convert into wealth. Attitude can make you happy or sad, loving or hateful, cheerful or remorseful, attractive or repulsive. Your attitude controls your very capacity and predisposition for success and prosperity.

Very few people claim full and total responsibility for the state of their lives, but instead give their personal powers and creative juices away by blaming the problems they face in life on the shortcomings of others, the state of the economy, their spouse, their boss, their domestic conditions, and any combination of a million other reasons they can conjure up in their minds. Or worse, the imagined shortcomings, they are convinced, exist in themselves. Do not allow yourself to be seduced into this destiny-altering state. Harness your personal power and God-given ability to engineer your own destiny by consciously controlling your attitude.

When you fully consider the impact your attitude has on your thoughts, perceptions, and actions, and the moment you become mindful of the awesome power that God has placed within you, you won't want to allow negative attitudes to sabotage your happiness, health, and success any longer. You will begin to nurture and groom your attitude and put it to positive use. It is a tool, a weapon, a treasure, and a contagion. Your attitude is more contagious than the most prolific disease ever faced by humankind. Its influence affects and impacts everything and everyone you come into contact with. It is a blessing you can share in any situation.

Your attitude determines the highs and lows of your life. It not only increases or decreases your emotional bank account but also the emotional assets of those around you. The state of your attitude determines the quality of your life. It colors your world. Groomed and nurtured in a positive manner, there will be no person or obstacle that can stand in the way of your success or fail to be impacted for the better.

I heard of a story about an elderly carpenter who was ready to retire. He told his employer of his plans to leave the house building business and live a more leisurely life with his wife and family. He would miss the paycheck, but he needed to retire. The contractor was sorry to see his good worker go and asked if he could build just one more house as a personal favor. The carpenter said he would, but in time it was easy to see that his heart was not in his work. He resorted to shoddy workmanship and used inferior materials. It was an unfortunate way to end his career. When the carpenter finished his work and the builder came to inspect the house, the employer handed the front-door key to the carpenter, saying, "This is your house. It is my gift to you."

What a shock! And what a shame! If he had only known he was building his own house he would have had a different attitude and done it all so differently. Now he had to live in the home he had built so sloppily.

So it is with us. We build our lives in a distracted way, reacting rather than acting, willing to tolerate less than the best. At important turning points and defining moments, we do not always put forth our best effort. Then, with a shock, we look at the situation we have created and find that we are now living in the house we have built. Many of us look back with regret. If we had only realized that every action we took or neglected to take in the past affected our future, we would have acted much differently. Think of yourself as the carpenter and your life as your house. Each day you hammer a nail, place a board, or erect a wall with your attitude. Build wisely, for it is the only life you will ever build.[61]

How could this be illustrated more clearly? Your life today is the result of your attitudes and choices. Take full and total responsibility for your attitude toward life, people, circumstances, and opportunities, because the reality you experience tomorrow will be the result of how you handled that responsibility today. With the right attitude, you can overcome all of the limits and obstacles set before you and live the life of your dreams.

If you serve Christ with this attitude, you will please God, and others will approve of you, too. —ROMANS 14:18 NLT

Let us therefore, as many as are perfect, have this attitude; and if in anything you have a different attitude, God will reveal that also to you. —PHILIPPIANS 3:15 NASB

Chapter 21

PERCEPTIONS

*It is one of the commonest of mistakes to consider that
the limit of our power of perception is also the limit
of all there is to perceive.* —C. W. LEADBEATER

*Blessed are they who see beautiful things in humble places
where other people see nothing.* —CAMILLE PISSARRO

Life is full of ambiguities. You often hear the question asked, "Is the glass half empty or half full?" as a metaphorical guide regarding how we look at life and perceive our realities. For indeed our perception is our reality. Jesus, when speaking to His disciples, simplifies for us how perception shapes and molds our lives. He said that our model for this is a child. The following story gives further insight into the principle of childlikeness.

One day, the father of a very wealthy family sent his son on a trip to the country with the express purpose of teaching him how poor people live. The young man spent a couple of days and nights on the farm of what would be considered a very poor family.

When he returned from his trip, the father asked his son, "Well, how was your trip? Did you see how poor people live?"

The son replied, "Oh yeah, I saw that we have one dog and they have four. We have a pool that reaches to the middle of our garden and they have a creek that has no end. We have imported lanterns in our garden and they have the stars at night. Our patio reaches to the front yard and they have the whole horizon. We have a small piece of land to live on and they have fields that go beyond our sight. We have servants who serve us, but they serve others. We buy our food, but they grow theirs. We have walls around our property to protect us; they have friends to protect them."

The boy's father was speechless. Then his son added, "Thanks, Dad, for showing me how poor we are."[62]

Isn't perspective a wonderful thing? It makes us wonder what would happen if we all gave thanks for everything we have instead of constantly worrying about what we don't have.

This story demonstrates how life can be perceived in much different ways. Perception is contextually created through our past experiences, which color our current experiences. Perception has to do with perspective, or how we see things and view life. In order for us to really benefit from our experience, sometimes we need to be able to see our lives and situations from eyes that are as pure as a child's. That is how God sees. God sees your life from the context of a completed work.

If you knew that God's plan for your life is to cause all things to work together for good (Romans 8:28), would you be willing to do more, to push through setbacks, and to attempt more in spite of the challenges you are currently facing? I have lived long enough to know that life awards and affords us all daily lessons and that nothing comes to us unless God allows it. I have learned to view every circumstance as a blessing from God; the good is an obvious blessing, but as I examine my life retrospectively, many things I perceived as bad somehow all worked together for my good as well. I am sure the same is true for you too.

Seeing life from a child's perspective simplifies everything. The captioned quote encourages me to put the awe back in my life and to see life from a positive perspective and not a negative one. In writing this section, I took some time to hang out with children. We caught butterflies, laughed at silly things, danced like no one was watching, and lay in the midst of wild flowers pointing out the shape of the clouds. I noticed that they never once talked about how bad the economy was or who did not believe in them, nor how they were going to get the money to pay for their next pair of socks. They absorbed their entire environment with the pureness of their heart and hopefulness of an untainted life.

Our examination of the clouds turned into a discussion of what they wanted to become when they grew up. Without hesitation they began to share, "When I grow up I..." Life had not thrown its curve balls yet, so their perception of selfhood and the unlimited potentiality that was divinely encrypted within their DNA became the context for their aspirations—not the current state of global affairs. If you dare to push through your current challenges with the innocence of a child and the experience of an adult, your proverbial life's glass will never be half empty, but always half full.

The Chinese language combines two symbols to express our English word *crisis*. One has to do with *danger* and the other with *opportunity*. Hidden within the crises and challenges with which you are currently confronted are opportunities. You alone have the responsibility to perceive them as something that threatens your success, prosperity, hopes, and dreams, or as the coming of a divine opportunity. Refuse to give your personal power away to circumstances and situations. Do not perceive yourself inept. You serve a God who is bigger than your circumstances; One who will empower you with the wisdom to overcome obstacles and to change your setbacks into setups.

In Genesis 26:1-31 Isaac was not only challenged by a global economic crises, but also by social and relational jealousy and opposition. Never once did he give his personal power away, but instead trusted God. The story ends on a high note with Isaac benefiting from his experience. Each challenge pushed him into his ultimate place of blessing. His perception of who God was, who he was, God's ability, and his ability caused him to triumph.

How do you perceive yourself? Do you allow others to determine your destiny or do you rely on God? Your perception, and yours alone, holds the key to your future.

Verily I say unto you, Whosoever shall not receive
the kingdom of God as a little child, he shall
not enter therein. —MARK 10:15 KJV

The Wombs of Vocation

GIVING BIRTH TO WHAT WE DO

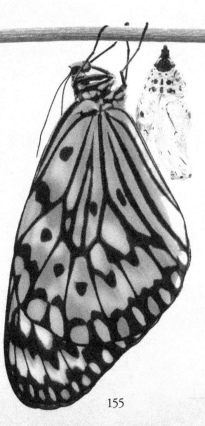

Chapter 22

HABITS

*We are what we repeatedly do. Excellence, then,
is not an act, but a habit.* —ARISTOTLE

*First we make our habits, then our habits
make us.* —CHARLES C. NOBLE

Everyone in the world has two things in common: good habits and bad habits. A habit is a conscious or unconscious activity that we do over and over again. These activities create our destiny. If you are not where you think you should be at this point in your life, check your habits. There are two habits I believe are particularly important to breaking through the success barrier, which most people don't usually place in the category of "habits." They are the habits of putting off until tomorrow what can be done today, and not following through—or rather, quitting too soon.

When it comes down to it, I think the very worst of all habits is what I have come to call the "*mañana* (tomorrow) habit," or procrastination. Procrastination is a very contagious and lethal character disease. Many of us who are infected with this condition may not even be fully aware of it. It took me awhile to put all its pieces together in my own life. When I understood what was at the root of my lack of success in a certain area, it was a big aha moment; and once the culprit was exposed, I could begin terminating it.

For years I battled taking off the extra weight I had acquired from traveling and eating late at night. Unlike most people, who are closet eaters, I am a social eater. Eighty percent of my time is spent in social settings. I can't resist trying new foods and exploring the creative culinary expressions of internationally acclaimed chefs and restaurants. Nor could I resist any invitation to dine out, no matter what the hour of the night. It's not that I don't have a wonderful eating plan and an awesome personal trainer. But once I hit the road, I could not seem to break the habit of social eating and eating late at night. I would repeatedly say to myself, "This week is the last week I am going to eat like this!" I had discipline in all other areas of my life except this one.

This is usually the case with many people. It is that one area you have to conquer. Since acquiring the particularly bad habit of eating late, I often heard myself saying, "This is the last time because *mañana* I will start my new eating plan." I have had this bad habit for a little while now, and my scale continues to remind me that I have not developed the eating habits of a champion. However, I am on my way. I am taking it one day at a time. The bad news is that it continues to be a daily struggle, at least for now. But the good news is that I've learned how to treat it and will teach you how you can kick the *mañana* habit too.

The secret to your success is hidden in your daily routine. Jenny Craig said, "It's not what you do once in a while, it's what you do day in and day out that makes the difference." My secret is simple. I now routinely commit to sticking to my goal for only twenty-four hours—just one, singular, solitary day. And this is what I do *every* day. I woke up this morning and said to myself, "You only have to stick to your eating plan for one day—and today is that day." I tell myself every morning that all I have to do is manage this one day, and this one day alone. You might be asking, "Is that it?" My response is, "Yes! That's it!" You can only work on eliminating your bad habits and establishing good habits one day at a time. Tell yourself, "I am going to stop drinking, smoking, lying, stealing, being late for work, overeating for one day—today." After all, today is all you really have to work with.

The other bad habit I mentioned is the habit of giving up too soon. Napoleon Hill said, "One of the most common causes of failure is the habit of quitting when one is overtaken by temporary defeat." We have all been guilty of giving up too soon at one time or another. But we can all work on developing the habit of pushing beyond the point of giving up every time we are tempted to quit. When you are tempted to give up, take a deep breath and push yourself to the next level. You can always do just a little more, hang on just a little longer, press in for just one more day. Theodore Roosevelt famously said,

> The credit belongs to those who are actually in the arena, who strive valiantly; who know the great enthusiasms, the great devotions, and spend themselves in a worthy cause; who at the best, know the triumph of high achievement; and who, at the worst, if they fail, fail while daring greatly, so that their place shall never be with those cold and timid souls who know neither victory nor defeat.[63]

Don't let the temptation to procrastinate or quit all together derail you. The only thing you should be putting off until tomorrow is quitting. Switch it around and say *"mañana"* when it comes to throwing in the towel, and then may that tomorrow never come!

Get in the habit of minding your habits one day at a time. Develop successful habits and successful habits will develop you. As Christopher Robin said to Pooh, "You're braver than you believe. Stronger than you seem. And smarter than you think." All that is keeping you where you are is a matter of habit. Just think, you could be one habit away from breaking through to your best possible future. Ask yourself, "What is the seed of potential residing in the womb of my habits?" I believe you'll be astounded by the answer!

> *Think of your sufferings as a weaning from that old sinful habit of always expecting to get your own way. Then you'll be able to live out your days free to pursue what God wants instead of being tyrannized by what you want.* —1 Peter 4:1-2 MSG

> *You're one happy man when you do what's right, one happy woman when you form the habit of justice.* —Psalm 106:3 MSG

Chapter 23

DECISIONS

Once you make a decision, the universe conspires to make it happen. —RALPH WALDO EMERSON

Your life changes the moment you make a new, congruent, and committed decision. —ANTHONY ROBBINS

Decisions determine destiny. —FREDERICK SPEAKMAN

It does not take much strength to do things, but it requires great strength to decide on what to do. —ELBERT HUBBARD

There lies within each of us a force of power that determines whether we succeed or fail. That force is our decision-making power. Failure, like success, is a matter of choice. Neither success nor failure is the result of a random set of coincidences determined by luck, fate, or right of birth. We are where we are today because of a series of decisions we chose or chose not to make over the course of all our yesterdays. In the timeless words of French philosopher and Nobel Prize winner Albert Camus, "Life is a sum of all your choices." And in the words of the ageless Professor Dumbledore of Harry Potter fame, "It is our choices, Harry, that show what we truly are, far more than our abilities."[64]

The desire to succeed at something lies within every person. And just like the grand tree lies asleep within an acorn, so does greatness lie within us all. There is a genius in every person waiting to be born or born again. Through this we face only two options: First, we make the decision to let the genius within remain asleep, or second, we choose to awaken that inner genius. "If you want to make your dreams come true," writes J. M. Power, "the first thing you have to do is wake up."

The word *genius* is a Latin word meaning "the guardian spirit of a person, spiritual inclination, wit, inborn nature."[65] Steven Pressfield, author of *The War of Art*, writes, "The Romans used it to denote an inner spirit, holy and inviolable, which watches over us, guiding us to our calling." He goes on to point out that "a writer writes with his genius; an artist paints with hers; everyone who creates operates from this sacramental center. It is our soul's seat, the vessel that holds our being-in-potential, our star's beacon and Polaris."[66]

Choosing to awaken your inner genius will lead you through life's great adventures and on to adventures in greatness. If you are complacent and allow your inner spirit to remain asleep, you will only act when acted upon; your life will be governed by the apathy of an automated stimulus-response and you will create nothing. However, if you choose to be proactive rather than reactive, you will become the Christopher Columbus of your dreams, goals, and vision, with a prosperous horizon forever stretching before you—a horizon of unlimited possibilities.

You are not barred from achieving greatness because of heredity, pedigree, or lack of education. If that were so, Jesus would never have become the Messiah. He was a poor carpenter's son from an obscure little town who was born in a barn of all places. Like Jesus, you can choose to pursue greatness regardless of where you were born or how you were brought up.

Nor are you prevented from accomplishing your goals or living the life of your dreams because of another person's estimation of your abilities. If that were true, there would be no Albert Einstein or Abraham Lincoln. You have not accomplished your goals, maximized your potential, written that book, started that business, or lost that weight only because you and you alone have decided not to. Forget about excuses. Anthony Robbins, a world famous motivational speaker, said it this way, "It is in your moments of decisions that your destiny is shaped."

Many times we do not make decisions that lead us closer to fulfilling the plans that God has for us because of deep feelings of inadequacy. But those feelings are nothing but lies and illusions. In the words of Marianne Williamson, "We were born to make manifest the glory of God that is within us. It's not just in some of us; it's in everyone. And as we let our own light shine, we unconsciously give other people permission to do the same."[67] Go ahead, make a decision to succeed, to fulfill your purpose, to maximize your potential—you are always only one decision away from living the life of your dreams.

Michael Miles, author of *Thirty Days to Change Your Life*, writes:

> The present is always fresh. There is always a new choice
> to make, and you are always creating your life again. No
> matter what has happened in the past—whatever habits you

have developed, however deeply ingrained are your patterns of behavior—there is always scope for you to choose a new response.[68]

Mary Anne Evans, better known as George Eliot, once wrote, "It is never too late to be who you might have been." And Anthony Robbins advises that you ask yourself, "How am I going to live today in order to create the tomorrow I'm committed to?" Begin today choosing to do the things required to be who you want to become. "Twenty years from now you will be more disappointed by the things that you didn't do than by the ones you did. So throw off the bowlines. Sail away from the safe harbor. Catch the trade winds in your sails. Explore. Dream. Discover."[69]

> *I have set before you life and death, blessing and cursing; therefore choose life, that both you and your descendants may live.* —DEUTERONOMY 30:19

Until one is committed
There is hesitancy, the chance to draw back,
Always ineffectiveness.
Concerning all acts of initiative (and creation),
There is one elementary truth,
The ignorance of which kills countless ideas
And splendid plans: That the moment one definitely
commits oneself,
Then Providence moves too.
All sorts of things occur to help one
That would never otherwise have occurred.
A whole stream of events issues from the decision
Raising in one's favor all manner
Of unforeseen incidents and meetings
And material assistance,
Which no man could have dreamt
Would have come his way.
I have learned a deep respect for one of Goethe's couplets:
Whatever you can do, or dream you can, begin it.
Boldness has genius and power in it.
—W. H. MURRAY, from *The Scottish*
Himalayan Expedition

Chapter 24

PURPOSE

I am here for a purpose and that purpose is to grow
into a mountain, not to shrink to a grain of sand.
Henceforth will I apply all my efforts to become the
highest mountain of all and I will strain my potential
until it cries for mercy. —OG MANDINO

We live in an age where people are attempting to discover their purpose and maximize their potential. Many believe they have a purpose in life but have not quite discovered exactly what it is. Usually when someone says they know what their purpose is in life, they are simply saying they were born for a reason, but what that reason is exactly may continue to elude them for the rest of their time here on earth. Author of the 1955 classic *Achieving Real Happiness*, Kenneth Hildebrand once said:

Multitudes of people, drifting aimlessly to and fro without a set purpose, deny themselves such fulfillment of their capacities, and the satisfying happiness which attends it. They are not wicked, they are only shallow. They are not mean or vicious; they simply are empty—shake them and they would rattle like gourds. They lack range, depth, and conviction. Without purpose their lives ultimately wander into the morass of dissatisfaction. As we harness our abilities to a steady purpose and undertake the long pull toward its accomplishment, rich compensations reward us. A sense of purpose simplifies life and therefore concentrates our abilities; and concentration adds power.[70]

Purpose allows you to get out of life's bleachers and play full out on the field of your dreams. God has a purpose for each one of our lives, and His purpose will prevail. Sometimes God will even mess up *our* plans so that only His purpose does prevail. Because it is God who decides our purpose in life, putting our life into His hands will guarantee that we will live a successful, on-purpose life. If that's all we do, we will have done well.

No matter what your circumstances are today, God has a beautiful purpose for your life. I came across this story about a cracked pot that perfectly illustrates this point:

> A water bearer in India had two large pots, which hung on each end of a pole that he carried across his neck. One of the pots had a crack in it, and while the other pot was perfect and always delivered a full portion of water at the end of the long walk from the stream to the master's house, the cracked pot arrived only half full.
>
> For a full two years this went on daily, with the bearer delivering only one and a half pots full of water to his master's

house. Of course, the perfect pot was proud of its accomplishments, but the poor cracked pot was tormented by its imperfections—ashamed that it was able to accomplish only half of what it had been made to do.

After two years of what it perceived to be a bitter failure, the cracked water pot spoke to the water bearer one day by the stream. "I am ashamed of myself, and I want to apologize to you." "Why?" asked the bearer, "What are you ashamed of?"

"I have only been able to deliver half my load because this crack in my side causes water to leak out all the way back to your master's house. You do all of this work and don't get full value for your efforts," the pot said. The water bearer patiently said to the pot, "As we return to the master's house I want you to notice the beautiful flowers along the path."

Indeed, as they went up the hill, the old cracked pot took notice of the beautiful wild flowers on the side of the path, and this cheered it some—but at the end of the trail, it still felt bad because it had leaked out half its load. Again it apologized to the bearer for its failure.

The bearer said to the pot, "Did you notice that there were flowers only on your side of the path but not on the other pot's side? That's because I have always known about your flaw, and I took advantage of it. I planted flower seeds on your side of the path, and every day while we walk back from the stream, you've watered them. Without you being just the way you are, my master would not have beautiful bouquets to grace his table."[71]

This story really spoke to me and let me know that purpose has a way of pushing through the most obstinate circumstances to find its truest expression. In the first chapter of the Gospel of Matthew, there is an account of the genealogy of Christ, which proves this point. God doesn't look at the outward appearance, but He speaks to potential; not where you are, but where you are going.

According to Matthew 1:1-17, purpose and sovereignty and divine destiny have the power to override and cancel the effect of the most horrible and dysfunctional of heredities, generational curses, imperfections, idiosyncratic insufficiencies, and humiliating histories. Although we may be tempted to skip the string of men and women mentioned in this text, and dismiss this account as antiquated Jewish writings or apostolic ramblings of no spiritual or applicable value (other than that of identifying the genealogical heritage of Jesus), a careful examination will expose divine eloquence in revealing that through the manifold background of Jesus (though divine in origin), His close relations with "common" men made Him the perfect candidate to bring redemption to humanity. Although truly God, He was also truly *of* man. Our human IQ is swallowed up in the divine "I AM." Our insufficiency is consumed by His all-sufficiency. He supplies all of our needs according to His riches in glory (Philippians 4:19).

God always fulfills His purpose irrespective of man's frailties. His purpose always prevails. He sees the end from the beginning. He chooses whom He uses. Just like the amazing men and women you read about in the Bible, God has impregnated you with greatness—with an assignment, a purpose, a mantle, an anointing, and a destiny. Your current circumstances will expose that divine encryption of greatness hidden within your DNA. So push! Push through your hard times, tears, trials, and setbacks!

The man by the pool of Bethesda lay there for thirty-eight years with the potential to walk locked up on the inside of him (John 5:5-8). He never did because no one spoke to his potential until Jesus came along and told him, "Rise up and walk!" I speak to your potential today. Whatever is hidden and lying dormant within you, I quicken it and call it forth. Today I want to encourage you not to give up and not to give in!

Remind yourself:

- God is about to come through for you.

- This is a day of good news.

- Your miracle is in motion.

- God is posturing you for greatness.

- The whole universe is rooting for you.

- Heaven is pregnant.

- The whole earth is groaning.

So will the real sons and daughters of God please stand up. Stand up in spite of your tears, your fears, your tests, and your struggles. Because when it is all over, you will live in new realms of power, influence, favor, and affluence. You'll be debt free, drama free, disease free, and depression free.

Heaven wants to deliver something through you and to you today. It is pregnant with the plans and purposes of God. Each of us has our own unique flaws. Battered, beaten, and worn out over the years, we often have the tendency to believe that somehow God's purpose cannot prevail in our lives. His purpose is stronger than our weaknesses, past failures, and present fears. We're all cracked pots! But if we will allow it, the Lord will use our flaws to grace His Father's table. In God's great economy, nothing goes to waste. Romans 9:19-23 states:

You will say to me then, "Why does He still find fault? For who has resisted His will?" But indeed, O man, who are you to reply against God? Will the thing formed say to him who formed it, "Why have you made me like this?" Does not the potter have power over the clay, from the same lump to make one vessel for honor and another for dishonor?

What if God, wanting to show His wrath and to make His power known, endured with much longsuffering the vessels of wrath prepared for destruction, and that He might make known the riches of His glory on the vessels of mercy, which He had prepared beforehand for glory?

As God calls you to the tasks He has appointed for you, don't be afraid of your flaws. Acknowledge them and allow Him to take advantage of them, and you too can be the cause of beauty in His pathway. Go out boldly, knowing that in your weakness you will find His strength. The Lord told Paul, *"My grace is sufficient for you, for My strength is made perfect in weakness"* (2 Corinthians 12:9).

He is the Potter and you are the clay. Paul inquired of the Romans, *"Does not the potter have power over the clay?"* (Romans 9:21). Of course He does. Let God's purpose prevail, as He chooses how He wants to use you in the earth.

This is the purpose that is purposed against the whole earth, and this is the hand that is stretched out over all the nations. For the Lord of hosts has purposed, and who will annul it? His hand is stretched out, and who will turn it back? —ISAIAH 14:26-27

Chapter 25

DETERMINATION

*Success is not final, failure is not fatal: it is the courage
to continue that counts.* —WINSTON CHURCHILL

*Failure will never overtake me if my determination
to succeed is strong enough.* —OG MANDINO

Napoleon Bonaparte, Emperor of France (1769–1821), said, "Impossible is a word only to be found in the dictionary of fools." In Matthew 19:26 Jesus said, *"With men this is impossible; but with God all things are possible."* What is considered impossible is truly a matter of opinion. As history shows, perseverance and determination often outweigh human notions of what is possible. In fact, determination is the critical ingredient of any worthwhile success. Nothing great has ever been achieved without it—no battle won, no business built, no barrier broken through, no bridge completed.

I want to share a true story that has been widely circulated about the building of the Brooklyn Bridge. The author is unknown, but it famously demonstrates the power of determination to overcome seemingly insurmountable odds:

> In 1883 a creative engineer named John Roebling was inspired to build a spectacular bridge connecting New York with Long Island. Bridge building experts throughout the world thought this was an impossible feat and told Roebling to forget the idea.
>
> Roebling could not ignore the vision he had in his mind of this glorious bridge. After much discussion and persuasion, he managed to convince his son Washington, an up-and-coming engineer, that the bridge in fact could be built.
>
> Working together for the first time, the father and son developed concepts of how it could be accomplished. With great excitement and anticipation, they hired their crew and began building the world's largest suspension bridge.
>
> The project started well, but when it was only a few months underway a tragic accident on the site took the life of John Roebling. Washington was injured and left paralyzed.
>
> In spite of his handicap Washington was never discouraged. All he could do was move one finger and decided to make the best use of it. He slowly developed a code of communication with his wife.
>
> He touched his wife's arm with that finger, indicating that he wanted her to call the engineers. Then he used the same method of tapping her arm to tell the engineers what to do. It seemed foolish but the project was under way again.

For thirteen years Washington tapped out his instructions with his finger on his wife's arm until the bridge was finally completed.

Today the spectacular Brooklyn Bridge stands as a tribute to the triumph of one man's indomitable spirit and his determination not to be defeated by circumstances.

Perhaps this is one of the best examples of overcoming physical odds to achieve an "impossible" goal. The belief of one man who was able to inspire the faith of others left a lasting tribute to the power of commitment and courage. Often the obstacles we face in our day-to-day life seem to loom larger than life, but our daily hurdles are really small in comparison to what others who have conquered the odds throughout history have faced. The Brooklyn Bridge shows us that dreams that seem impossible can be realized with determination and persistence, no matter the odds.

If you are holding this book and reading it, you probably have all your fingers. What is preventing *you* from "tapping out" your vision and dreams? When your reach seems to exceed your grasp, this story should remind you that even the most distant dream can be realized with determination and persistence. And remember, *"Nothing is impossible with God."* With a little help from above and a little faith in your heart, there is nothing impossible for you. So push!

Press toward the mark for the prize of the high calling of God in Christ Jesus. —PHILIPPIANS 3:14 KJV

Anything is possible if a person believes. —MARK 9:23 NLT

Don't Quit

By Edgar A. Guest

When things go wrong, as they sometimes will,
when the road you're trudging seems all uphill,
when the funds are low and the debts are high,
and you want to smile but you have to sigh,
when care is pressing you down a bit –
rest if you must,
but don't you quit.
Life is queer with its twists and turns.
As every one of us sometimes learns.
And many a fellow turns about
when he might have won had he stuck it out.
Don't give up though the pace seems slow –
you may succeed with another blow.
Often the goal is nearer than
it seems to a faint and faltering man;
Often the struggler has given up
when he might have captured the victor's cup;
and he learned too late when the night came down,
how close he was to the golden crown.
Success is failure turned inside out –
the silver tint of the clouds of doubt,
and when you never can tell how close you are,
it may be near when it seems afar;
so stick to the fight when you're hardest hit -
it's when things seem worst,
you must not quit.

Chapter 26

WORK

*We can do no great things, only small things
with great love.* —MOTHER TERESA

People often say a person is lucky when he or she achieves something notable, makes a scientific breakthrough, writes a brilliant best-seller, breaks a longstanding record, rises to the top of their game, distinguishes themselves in a specific discipline, receives accolades for the successful completion of an assignment, starts a prosperous business, or accomplishes anything at all. They feel that these are people who have gotten all of the breaks at the exclusion of everyone else.

In reality, neither "lucky breaks" nor "fate" have anything to do with success and prosperity. Luck is not an ingredient in the secret formula for success. So-called "luck" is usually found at the exact junction where preparation, diligence, and hard work intersect with needs, problems, and opportunity. For a time, an individual may get ahead by "pulling strings" or dropping names, but eventually someone with discipline, consistency, and passion will displace him or her.

Success, prosperity, and great accomplishments are not the results of a fortuitous plethora of lucky stars bestowed upon these individuals at birth. Instead, they are the direct results of a series of deliberate activities these people undertake and disciplined steps they consistently make, lit by the kindling of drive, determination, and passion. These are the winning attributes that lock shoulders to the grindstone of hard work.

Diligence and persistence are the primary ingredients of the "secret formula" that fuels their drive and enables them to push past the thresholds of pain, fatigue, and discouragement in order to realize their dreams and accomplish their goals. The world, however, is moved along not only by the mighty shoves of its heroes, but also by the aggregate of the tiny pushes of each honest worker. Helen Keller said, "I long to accomplish great and noble tasks, but it is my chief duty to accomplish humble tasks as though they were great and noble."

In the Garden of Eden, the first assignment given to man was to work. He did not have a car note, mortgage, school fees, utility expenses, or cell phone bills. Therefore, work was not associated with something that was unpleasant. Work was a means by which he could maximize his potential while securing wealth, luxury, and extravagance.

In the seventeenth century, Francoise de Motteville wrote in her memoirs, "The true way to render ourselves happy is to love our work and find in it our pleasure." Frank Lloyd Wright once said, "I know the price of success: dedication, hard work, and an unremitting devotion to the things you want to see happen." Because ability has no value without opportunity, it is therefore the opportunity to work that gives us our truest success. Ephesians 5:16 tells us to *"make the most of every opportunity"* (NLT). And we read in Proverbs 22:29: *"Do you see a man who excels in his work? He will stand before kings; he will not stand before unknown men."*

Power is manifested in potential. Just like a tree sleeps in an acorn and a house awaits its day of manifestation asleep in the limbs of a tree, so do your business ideas, books, and ground-breaking discoveries lie dormant within the womb of potential. Adam was given the potential to become a world leader and millionaire. He had only begun to maximize his potential through the work he engaged in. What is the seed of potential waiting to be birthed through your power to work?

Adam accomplished his assignment because of the glory (anointing) that was permanently upon him. Because of that anointing, he was equipped with the capacity to give (and remember) the names of *"all cattle, to the birds of the air, and to every beast of the field"* (Genesis 2:20). Work was God's divine opportunity presented to him in order to maximize his potential and mandate. Through God's divine challenge to name every living creature, Adam became industrious and resourceful—he tapped into his potential. With the knowledge acquired from his experience, Adam was able to perceive truth from error, develop self-discipline, and persevere with confidence because he was achieving God's original mandate for his life. He was prosperous and successful through his God-given creativity, imagination, and industry.

Challenges were divinely given to Adam to maximize his potential. As he rose to the challenge, latent abilities and talents were activated. The Garden of Eden became Adam's laboratory for personal growth, economic development, and educational reform. Adam discovered that the greatest secret to success was to expand his knowledge and stretch his mind. He was diligent to work his mind and then to follow through with his work mindfully. He was never underemployed or unemployed.

The solution to unemployment is work. Sometimes when we lose our jobs, we have been given a divine opportunity to work… our minds, that is. Set your mind to work on manifesting the divine potential inherent in your power to work.

> *But thou shalt remember the Lord thy God: for it is He that giveth thee power to get wealth, that He may establish His covenant which He swear unto thy fathers, as it is this day.* —DEUTERONOMY 8:18 KJV

The Wombs of Destiny

GIVING BIRTH TO YOUR DIVINE POTENTIAL

Chapter 27

RELATIONSHIPS

*The true sense of community lies in understanding our
interconnectedness and acting from a sense of relatedness.
It is a challenge. Let's begin at the beginning. That is
where we can start to reweave the sacred web of life so
that it once again becomes whole.* —SUZANNE ARMS

*Some people come into our lives and quickly go. Some
stay for a while, leave footprints on our hearts, and
we are never, ever the same.* —FLAVIA WEEDN

Charles Plumb was a U.S. Navy jet pilot in Vietnam. After
seventy-five combat missions, his plane was destroyed by a surface-to-air missile. Plumb ejected and parachuted into enemy hands.
He was captured and spent six years in a communist Vietnamese
prison. One day, decades later, when Plumb and his wife were sitting
in a restaurant, a man from another table came up and said, "You're

Plumb! You flew jet fighters in Vietnam from the aircraft carrier *Kitty Hawk*. You were shot down!"

"How in the world did you know that?" asked Plumb.

"I packed your parachute," the man replied. Plumb gasped in surprise and gratitude. The man pumped his hand and said, "I guess it worked!"

Plumb assured him, "It sure did. If your chute hadn't worked, I wouldn't be here today."

Plumb couldn't sleep that night, thinking about the man he met that day at the restaurant. He kept wondering what he had looked like in a Navy uniform: a white hat, a bib in the back, and bell-bottom trousers. He wondered how many times he might have seen him and never said, "Good morning," or asked, "How are you?" because he was a fighter pilot and that man was just a sailor. Plumb thought of the many hours the sailor had spent at a long wooden table in the bowels of the ship, carefully weaving the shrouds and folding the silks of each individual parachute—each time holding in his hands the fate of someone he didn't know.

Who's packing your parachute? Every successful person has someone who has their back and helps provide what they need to make it through the day. This is the power of relationship. Who do you have in your life making sure you have a properly packed parachute?

Not only that, when you are shot down over enemy territory, you'll need several kinds of parachutes ready to open and convey you to safety. When your life is hanging in the balance, you will need to rely on physical, mental, emotional, and spiritual parachutes. You will need all of these to reach safety. Who within your relational constellation can you rely on to pack each of these parachutes?

Life often throws us curve balls and surface-to-air missiles that can bring us into emotional, mental, and spiritual lows. In order to survive, we need to recognize, acknowledge, and thank those individuals in our lives for providing us a functional parachute. If you do not have those kinds of people in your life, pray and ask God to send them. Remember, though, you must become a parachute maker for others too, because those who will have friends must show themselves friendly (Proverbs 18:24).

Genuine relationships are important. There is an art for building them and a recipe for maintaining them. Let's take a closer look at the elements needed to pack a life-worthy parachute that will carry you to safety when you are shot down.

LOVE

In the Bible, Paul pointed out that life without love is worthless. Love is the ultimate reason why we are all created. Relationships are based on love. In fact, God's relationship with the human race is based on love too: *"God so love the world that He gave His only begotten Son"* (John 3:16). Certainly, this is the greatest expression of love ever. This kind of love is not based on feelings; it is a decision that requires sacrifice. Love is your commitment to the people important to you; it is unselfishly giving up what you have for the benefit of someone else.

According to Oliver Wendell Holmes, "Love is the master key that opens the gates of happiness." Any relationship built upon love weathers the harsh challenges of this human life. We know that *"if we love one another, God abides in us, and His love has been perfected in us"* (1 John 4:12). Now that is a powerful thought!

HONESTY

If love is the foundation, then honesty is the framework of any quality relationship. For a loving relationship to succeed, sincerity, honesty, transparency, and openness are a must. A relationship seasoned with lies, misrepresentations of truth, or deception will never grow. Honesty is the only thing that sustains and feeds a truly life-giving relationship.

Honesty evolves out of personal integrity. I have learned that integrity is telling myself the truth while honesty is telling the truth to others. You must be honest with yourself and with others—if you are not, you are compromising your relationship with God.

TRUST

"I trust you." These three words carry almost as much weight as "I love you." In fact, they are almost synonymous. When we commit to developing a trusting relationship, we must let down our guards, walls, and fences so that other people see our vulnerability, and that can be very difficult and uncomfortable. But when we learn to trust at a deep level, we open up, let others see our wounds and fears, and allow them to help in the healing process—and vice versa. When people bestow their trust upon you, based on genuine love and honesty, you must do everything in your power not to break that trust. Once you do, you may attempt to piece your relationship back together again, but as with glass or china, you will always see the crack.

RESPECT

Respect begets respect. It is the key to nurturing an honest, durable relationship. But you must first respect yourself. Eighteenth-century novelist and clergyman Laurence Sterne once said, "Respect for ourselves guides our morals, respect for others guides our manners." Regardless of your shortcomings or the shortcomings of others, respect is a virtue that will give any relationship sustainability. Demonstrate respect for other people's rights, opinions, personhood, possessions, and boundaries, and expect them to do the same for you.

A Serving Heart

Having a serving heart requires you to put the needs of others above your own: *"in honor giving preference to one another"* (Romans 12:10). Servanthood is the precursor to achieving a rich and rewarding relationship.

Communication

Interaction and exchange of ideas is very important in keeping a healthy and genuine relationship. It is how we let others know our feelings, thoughts, and views and how we express compassion for one another. When we communicate with someone, we are connecting with him or her on an emotional level. We allow ourselves to feel what they feel, to understand their thoughts, and see what they want us to see. Our ability to share and connect with others in a deep and meaningful way is one of life's greatest joys and one of God's most precious gifts.

Commitment

Commitment is a prerequisite to any relationship. It is our loyalty, devotion, and dedication to someone dear to us. Commitment says, "I know you have weaknesses, and sometimes you will disappoint me and I will disappoint you, but I am in this relationship because I love you, all of you, weaknesses and all. Through thick and thin, sun and rain, hardship and pain, I am here for you."

Forbearance and Forgiveness

I call these the twin virtues. We must be patient with those we are in relationship with. Remember that sometimes challenging relational circumstances are intentionally delegated to us as a divine gift so that we have the opportunity to grow. It is what makes us and our relationships stronger. When we recognize our flaws, this helps us to become more understanding, patient, and forgiving with one another.

Forgiveness is a heartfelt decision to let go of the past and forget about the pain you've been caused. Learn how to forgive yourself for the dumb things you do and how to forgive others for the dumb things they do too. We are all susceptible to bouts of bad judgment.

LOYALTY/FAITHFULNESS

This is what I call the "stick-to-it" component of relationships. Many relationships falter because they lack loyalty. Marriages fail because of unfaithfulness. Husbands and wives forget what they've pledged to each other at the altar. Business partnerships and friendships are ruined because of treachery and betrayal. We switch friends and change boyfriends and girlfriends like we're changing shirts. However, there are times when we just have to stick around, commit ourselves to being loyal, and allow our relationships to move forward. A "stick-to-it" attitude when it comes to relationships will position us to withstand the challenges of life.

KINDNESS

Treat every person you meet as if he or she were a friend, whether or not they have earned it. You never know how that person might be a blessing to you someday. As the writer of Hebrews put it, *"Do not forget to entertain strangers, for by so doing some have unwittingly entertained angels"* (Hebrews 13:2). Being kind is an easy way to guarantee you don't sabotage your own success.

HUMOR

Humor is a very good healing tool in a relationship, and laughter is good for the soul. When things are tense, a good laugh always proves a potent relaxant. It adds zest to serious business deals, brings fun and enjoyment to relationships, and strengthens the bonds of teamwork within corporate environments. When someone cracks a funny joke in a room, everybody who hears it can't help but laugh or smile. Funny memories make our lives unforgettably sweet.

The laughs I've shared with friends in high school and college have often come to mind, and every time they do I can't help but smile at the memory. Laughter is the most cost effective do-it-yourself face-lift a person can have. And it's incredibly contagious. Wear a smile whenever possible because it *always* makes you look better and makes everyone around you feel better.

Fostering good relationships is not automatic. You must work at it daily. These are the things that a good relational parachute is made out of. I ask you once again, "Who is packing your parachute?" Choose and then build your relationships carefully.

He who is of a merry heart has a continual
feast. —PROVERBS 15:15

Chapter 28

REJECTION

*I think all great innovations are built on
rejections.* —Louis Ferdinand Celine

*I take rejection as someone blowing a bugle
in my ear to wake me up and get going rather
than retreat.* —Sylvester Stallone

Rejection is one of those life experiences from which we usually don't see how we can benefit. However, as I studied the lives of successful people, I discovered that most of them had something in common—many of them had experienced rejection. We don't have to look far in the Bible to see the same is true of the great patriarchs of the faith. Joseph, for example, was hated and rejected by his siblings, falsely accused for a crime he never committed, and imprisoned. Yet he went on to become prime minister of Egypt. Moses was an ex-convict with a speech impediment. In spite of his handicap, his past, and being rejected by his own people, he eventually became a world-class leader and reformer.

What about modern heroes of the faith? Oral Roberts suffered from the socially crippling effects of stuttering as a child. Abraham Lincoln was told he was too poor and did not have enough education to run for president. Look at our cultural heroes such as George Lucas, who spent four years shipping the script for *Star Wars* around to the various studios and racking up numerous rejections in the process. Walt Disney was turned down for a loan by over a hundred banks before he secured funding to develop Disneyland. He was also fired from his job at a newspaper for "lacking ideas."

Lou Ferrigno, best known for his role on the TV show *The Incredible Hulk,* suffered rejection from his father because of chronic ear infections that resulted in hearing loss. His father believed that he would never achieve success, yet Lou went on at the age of twenty to become the youngest bodybuilder ever to win the Mr. Universe title. "If I hadn't lost my hearing," Lou said, "I wouldn't be where I am now. It forced me to maximize my potential. I had to be better than the average person to succeed."[72] Even Michael Jordan was cut from his high school basketball team. Michael said, "I've failed over and over again in my life, and that is why I succeed." Beethoven's music teacher told him he was a hopeless composer. At four years of age, and partially deaf in one ear, Thomas Edison was sent home from school with a note saying he was too stupid to learn. With only three months of formal education, Edison went on to become one of the world's greatest inventors.

Rejection is a divine announcement that you were never supposed to prosper within a particular relationship or realm. Did you see the movie blockbuster *The Pursuit of Happyness,* starring Will Smith?

The movie is based on the true rags-to-riches story of Chris Gardner. You know you've made it when Will Smith is portraying you in a biographical movie.

In and out of foster care as a child, this entrepreneur, whose net worth was estimated at $65 million in 2006, lost his wife and was homeless on the streets of San Francisco with a young son in the early 1980s. Determined to make it as a stockbroker, he took a position as a trainee at Dean Witter Reynolds. With little money, Gardner and his son slept in parks and public restrooms after Gardner worked as many hours as he could, pro bono, to become the top banker at his firm. It all paid off in 1987 when Gardner started his own brokerage firm in Chicago.

Look at your life from a different perspective. Perhaps your past rejections are the divine push you need to move on to bigger and better things.

Your words stand fast and true; rejection doesn't faze You. —ROMANS 3:4 MSG

But the rejection will force honesty, as God reveals who they really are. —LUKE 2:35 MSG

Chapter 29

FAILURE

A failure is not always a mistake; it may simply be
the best one can do under the circumstances. The
real mistake is to stop trying. —B. F. Skinner

One of man's greatest fears is the fear of failure. However, learning from failure is part of the process of being successful. History's most successful figures could not have accomplished what they did had they not embraced the lessons failure offered them or had they heeded the deceptive voices of the fear of failure. Fear can be defined as "False Evidence Appearing Real." Fear is only a matter of perception, as is the concept of failure. What some see as failure and an obstacle, others see as a learning opportunity and stepping stone.

Failure is really success turned inside out. It is God's gentle way of saying, "Don't give up; try another way." You don't fail because your efforts are unsuccessful; you fail only when you give up or give in. The famous dramatist Tennessee Williams said, "I have always been pushed by the negative. The apparent failure of a play sends me back to my typewriter that very night, before the reviews are out. I am more compelled to get back to work than if I had a success." Thomas Edison said, "Many of life's failures are people who did not realize how close they were to success when they gave up. Remember, you have not lived if you never failed." And Lou Holtz said, "I think everyone should experience defeat at least once during their career. You learn a lot from it."

It was Winston Churchill who, having failed the sixth grade, was later defeated in every election for public office until he became prime minister at the age of sixty-two. He later wrote, "Never give in, never give in, never, never, never, never—in nothing, great or small, large or petty—never give in except to convictions of honor and good sense. Never, never, never, never give up." Churchill must have taken his cues from another one of history's most admired political figures, Abraham Lincoln.

As a young man, Lincoln went to war a captain and returned a private. He later failed at business. As a lawyer in Springfield, he was too impractical and temperamental to keep his law practice afloat. He turned to politics and was defeated in his first try for the legislature, again defeated in his first attempt to be nominated for congress, defeated in his application to be commissioner of the General Land Office, defeated in the senatorial election of 1854, defeated in his efforts for the vice presidency in 1856, and defeated in the senatorial election of 1858. At about that time, he wrote in a letter to a friend, saying, "I am now the most miserable man living. If what I feel were equally distributed to the whole human family, there would not be one cheerful face on the earth." He went on to become one of the greatest U.S. presidents in American history.

Repeated failure is the hallmark of the world's great politicians, businesspeople, artists, inventors, and athletes. After four years on a whaling ship, R. H. Macy took his hard-earned, diligently saved money and opened his own thread and needle shop in Boston, Massachusetts. The store failed less than a year later. He tried again—in fact, several times over—only to fail over and over again. One hundred and fifty years later, Macy's continues with more than 850 stores across the United States, Puerto Rico, and Guam.[73]

Thomas Edison's teachers said he was "too stupid to learn anything." He was fired from his first two jobs for being "non-productive." As an inventor, Edison made over a thousand unsuccessful attempts at inventing the light bulb. When an aide urged him to quit after several hundred failures, he replied, "Why quit now? We know of at least a hundred things that won't work." When a reporter asked him how it felt to fail a thousand times, Edison replied, "I didn't fail a thousand times. The light bulb was an invention with a thousand steps."

Most of us have heard of Babe Ruth who set a record with 714 home runs in his baseball career. But few remember he struck out 1,330 times on the way to that record. Most people know that Jonas Salk discovered the polio vaccine, but few realize he had to fail two hundred times before he found the right one. Nearly everyone who watches professional basketball agrees Michael Jordan is one of the greatest players of all time, but most people don't realize he failed to make the basketball team his sophomore year in high school.

I have learned to view my perceived failures as a challenge to try the same thing another way or to modify my approach and perspective. In so doing, I not only grew wiser, but the outcome was also far better than I initially anticipated. God orchestrates certain defeats, setbacks, and failures so that eventually we experience the most victorious lives possible. The human spirit is never finished when it is defeated or when it fails in its efforts to succeed—it is only finished when it fails in its resolve, never to try again. As Henry Ford once said, "One who fears failure limits his activities. Failure is only the opportunity to more intelligently begin again."

Like many who have gone before us, your life's experiences, successes, and yes, failures eventually become testimonies, biographies, and histories that inspire others to press on until their dreams become reality. Because we are surrounded by so many examples of faith, we must get rid of everything that slows us down, especially sin that distracts us. We must run the race that lies ahead of us and never, never, never give up (Hebrews 12:1).

> *The godly may trip seven times, but they will get up again.* —PROVERBS 24:16 NLT

Chapter 30

TIME

*Time is the most undefinable yet paradoxical of
things; the past is gone, the future is not come, and
the present becomes the past even while we attempt
to define it, and, like the flash of lightning, at once
exists and expires.* —CHARLES CALEB COLTON

*Time is a great teacher, but unfortunately it kills
all its pupils.* —LOUIS HECTOR BERLIOZ

Lee Iacocca, a twentieth-century businessman, said, "The ability to concentrate and to use your time well is everything if you want to succeed." One of the most important questions one can ask themselves when it comes to time is, "What is the most important thing I can do with the time I've been given?" Look at what Colossians 4:5 tells us, *"Behave yourselves wisely [living prudently and with discretion]...making the very most of the time"* (AMP). If you plan to achieve more, accomplish more, and do more, you must learn to behave yourself wisely by *first* eliminating time-wasters.

Like the enemy himself, time-wasters do nothing but kill, steal, and destroy your life. I like what the early eighteenth-century English cleric Charles Caleb Colton has been quoted as saying, "Much may be done in those little shreds and patches of time which every day produces, and which most men throw away." And people during that time didn't even have the distraction of electronics! Look at the time-wasters we must learn to negotiate today.

TELEVISION

According to a recent survey of the A. C. Nielsen Company, the average American watches more than four hours of television every day.[74] This information can be translated to twenty-eight hours of television viewing per week, which in turn means about two months a year. In a sixty-five-year life span, people spend and average of nine years glued to the television set. Instead of sitting in front of the television set watching sitcoms and reality shows, refocus your attention, energy, and resources for the accomplishment of what truly matters to you—your priorities. Live life; don't watch someone else's go by.

Overcome your television addiction by getting rid of the television set. Yes, you read me right: Get rid of it! In our own household, we don't have televisions in the main living areas or bedrooms. We do have a vast library and other reading materials that feed our mind instead of sapping it. This is one of my secrets to accomplishing so many things.

However, if getting rid of that state-of-the-art flat screen television is just too much for you, then learn now to cut back your viewing hours. Believe me—you can survive without your favorite shows. Try reading for a change. Books enhance your imagination and actually help you create more vivid pictures in your mind than watching television shows.

Telephone Calls

The telephone is a very ingenious invention and I personally thank Mr. Bell for making it possible. However, it has its own share of disadvantages. Telephone calls can be an annoying and constant source of interruption. Whether you're working, reading, visiting with someone, or meditating, when the phone rings it breaks your focus.

Practice personal mastery of the phone. Before attending any meeting or immersing yourself in your work, set your phone on silent. Let your voice messaging system accept all of your calls. Review your messages only after you have finished with your work or meeting. You can return the calls of the most important callers. This way, you can still receive your calls and, at the same time, screen not-so-important phone calls without answering them. When you do return the calls, keep the conversation short and straight to the point. Remember, the person on the other end is probably not welcoming the interruption either.

It's the little interruptions and small portions of stolen time that add up to missed opportunities. "One must learn a different sense of time, one that depends more on small amounts than big ones," advised Sister Mary Paul.

Internet

The Internet in general is overwhelmingly awesome, especially for younger folks and their yuppie counterparts. If the telephone allows people to communicate more easily, than the Internet makes the world smaller and draws people closer together—maybe not physically, but certainly mentally. Regular mail has been replaced by instant messaging, reaching people anywhere around the globe. Online chatting lets strangers engage in cyber conversations without even seeing each other in person. Virtual social networking and blogging allows the general public to know your thoughts and opinions and gives a peek into your private life through posted photos and videos.

Aren't these things awesome? Yes, they are. That is the reason why we are all so hooked on them. We don't only watch television at home, but we also browse the web wherever we are thanks to wireless technology. We can download music, videos, movies, games, etc. The fact that we sit in front of our computer and browse the web for hours, even when we're at work, diverts us from doing the things that are most important to us. This is when the Internet intercepts our focus from our goals.

With all that being said, how can you break through these barriers? It is only by means of a potent combination of focus, self-discipline, and determination that we can unblock our road to success and prosperity. One way to do that is to develop your emotional intelligence—or EQ—by practicing the art of delaying gratification. In other words, do the hard work now in order to enjoy the taste of the sweet fruit later. Plant now; reap later. This is an age-old, simple truth. Learn to wait for it because discipline always delivers in good time. It was the late sixteenth-century mathematician and astronomer Johannes Kepler who so wisely said, "Truth is the daughter of time, and I feel no shame in being her midwife."

The Book of James tell us to *"let endurance and steadfastness and patience have full play and do a thorough work, so that you may be [people] perfectly and fully developed [with no defects], lacking in nothing"* (James 1:4 AMP). Patience is cultivated through focus, self-discipline, and determination. Find in yourself what you are passionate about.

Regardless of your chosen career, learn to love what you do and motivate yourself. And for everything that you decide to accomplish, delay your gratification. This is how you can have quality time to fulfill your goals in life and harvest the sweet fruits of your labor: *"To everything there is a season, a time for every purpose"* (Ecclesiastes 3:1). Do not abort your purpose by wasting or rushing time.

> *My words are of a kind which will be fulfilled in the appointed and proper time.* (Luke 1:20 AMP)

> *For the vision is yet for the appointed time; it hastens toward the goal and it will not fail. Though it tarries, wait for it; for it will certainly come, it will not delay.* (Habakkuk 2:3 NASB)

I want to leave you with this story called, "Thanks for Your Time:"

It had been some time since Jack had seen the old man; college, girls, career, and life itself got in the way. In fact, Jack moved clear across the country in pursuit of his dreams. There, in the rush of his busy life, Jack had little time to think about the past and often no time to spend with his wife and son. He was working on his future and nothing could stop him.

Over the phone, his mother told him, "Mr. Belser died last night. The funeral is Wednesday." Memories flashed through his mind like an old newsreel as he sat quietly remembering his childhood days. "Jack, did you hear me?"

"Oh, sorry, Mom. Yes, I heard you. It's been so long since I thought of him. I'm sorry, but I honestly thought he died years ago," Jack said.

"Well, he didn't forget you. Every time I saw him he'd ask how you were doing. He'd reminisce about the many days you spent over 'his side of the fence' as he put it," Mom told him.

"I loved that old house he lived in," Jack said.

"You know, Jack, after your father died, Mr. Belser stepped in to make sure you had a man's influence in your life," she said.

"He's the one who taught me carpentry," he said. "I wouldn't be in this business if it weren't for him. He spent a lot of time teaching me things he thought were important. Mom, I'll be there for the funeral," Jack promised.

As busy as he was, he kept his word. Jack caught the next flight to his hometown. Mr. Belser's funeral was small and uneventful. He had no children of his own, and most of his relatives had passed away.

The night before he had to return home, Jack and his Mom stopped by to see the old house next door one more time. Standing in the doorway, Jack paused for a moment. It was like crossing over into another dimension, a leap through space and time. The house was exactly as he remembered. Every step held memories. Every picture, every piece of furniture…Jack stopped suddenly.

"What's wrong, Jack?" his Mom asked.

"The box is gone," he said.

"What box?" Mom asked.

"There was a small gold box that he kept locked on top of his desk. I must have asked him a thousand times what was inside. All he'd ever tell me was, 'The thing I value most,'" Jack said.

It was gone. Everything about the house was exactly how Jack remembered it, except for the box. He figured someone from the Belser family had taken it. "Now I'll never know what was so valuable to him," Jack thought.

It had been about two weeks since Mr. Belser died. Returning home from work one day Jack discovered a note in his mailbox. "Signature required on a package. No one at home. Please stop by the main post office within the next three days," the note read.

Early the next day Jack retrieved the package. The small box was old and looked like it had been mailed a hundred years ago. The handwriting was difficult to read, but the return address caught his attention. "Mr. Harold Belser," it read.

Jack took the box out to his car and ripped open the package. There inside was the gold box and an envelope. Jack's hands shook as he read the note inside. "Upon my death, please forward this box and its contents to Jack Bennett. It's the thing I valued most in my life."

A small key was taped to the letter. His heart racing, as tears filling his eyes, Jack carefully unlocked the box. There inside he found a beautiful gold pocket watch. Running his fingers slowly over the finely etched casing, he unlatched the cover. Inside he found these words engraved: "Jack, Thanks for your time! —Harold Belser."

"The thing he valued most was my time," Jack said to himself.

Jack held the watch for a few minutes, then called his office and cleared his appointments for the next two days.

"Why?" Janet, his assistant, asked.

"I need some time to spend with my son," he said. "Oh, by the way, Janet, thanks for your time!" [75]

As Maya Angelou so aptly quoted, "Life is not measured by the number of breaths we take, but by the moments that take our breath away." Time is indeed precious and how you choose to spend it is important.

> *See then that you walk circumspectly, not as*
> *fools but as wise, redeeming the time, because*
> *the days are evil.* —EPHESIANS 5:15-16

YESTERDAY, TODAY, TOMORROW

There are two days in every week about which we should not
worry.
Two days which should be kept free from fear and apprehension.
One of these days is yesterday with its mistakes and cares,
Its faults and blunders, its aches and pains.
Yesterday has passed forever beyond our control.
All the money in the world cannot bring back yesterday.
We cannot undo a single act we performed,
We cannot erase a single word we said. Yesterday is gone.
The other day we should not worry about is tomorrow.
With its possible adversities, its burdens,
Its large promise and poor performance.
Tomorrow is also beyond our immediate control.
Tomorrow's sun will rise, either in splendor or
behind a mask of clouds,
but it will rise.
Until it does, we have no stake in tomorrow, for it is yet unborn.
This just leaves only one day...Today.

Any person can fight the battles of just one day.
It is only when you and I add the burdens
of those two awful eternities—
yesterday and tomorrow that we break down.
It is not the experience of today that drives people mad.
It is the remorse or bitterness for something
which happened yesterday
and the dread of what tomorrow may bring.
Let us therefore live but one day at a time.
—AUTHOR UNKNOWN (**Possible author Jennifer** Kitsch)[76]

Chapter 31

THE MORNING

I love the sweet smell of dawn –
our unique daily opportunity to smell time,
to smell opportunity –
each morning being a new beginning.
—EMME WOODHULL-BÄCHE

Every morning is the dawning of a new day, and with it the dawning of new opportunities to win, to succeed, to maximize your potential, to accomplish your goals, and to realize your dreams. Today is the only day you will ever have. Yesterday is gone and tomorrow will never come, for when it does, it will be today. You only have one decision to make, and that is how you will make the most of the present. The morning is the seedling for the rest of your day.

I came across this quote the other day by J. M. Power: "If you want to make your dreams come true, the first thing you have to do is wake up." The greatest achievements in life occur when someone wakes up from a dream and makes that dream a reality. There are things that are asleep within your soul. The next best-selling novel, the next great concerto, or the next great invention; the next great politician, scientist, or hero is asleep within you. Wake up that sleeping giant within. The great oak tree had to be stirred to life from within the tiny acorn. What lies dormant within you, just waiting to be stirred to life? Give birth to the champion, push out the inventor, wake up the scientist; unleash the artist, activist, or author you are called to be. Wake up that sleeping giant. It is your time to rise and shine.

THE BREAKFAST OF CHAMPIONS

If you want to succeed in life, you must acquire the appetite of a champion. They hunger and thirst for success. Champions get their day started with achievement affirmations and declarations as part of their daily regimen of mental supplements. They do not allow destiny-altering thoughts to enter their mind or feed on negativity of any kind. They eliminate toxic thoughts and words from their mental and verbal diet.

They do not procrastinate or leave things until tomorrow. Champions do what needs to be done today. They rise in the morning on purpose, for a purpose, and to complete their purpose. They know that you can't put off your purpose until tomorrow or you will never fulfill it. What else do champions do? Below are listed the most common characteristics of champions.

CHAMPIONS KNOW HOW TO FACE THEIR FEARS

Are you frightened of failure? Do you fear success and the consequences of it? Are you scared of what other people might say about you? Are you terrified of what you are capable of? Is it the unknown of the future or your past experiences that hold you back? Don't allow fear to overpower you. Allow these words of Marianne Williamson to sink into your consciousness:

> Our deepest fear is not that we are inadequate. Our deepest fear is that we are powerful beyond measure. It is our light, not our darkness that most frightens us. We ask ourselves, "Who am I to be brilliant, gorgeous, talented, fabulous?" Actually, who are you not to be? You are a child of God. Your playing small does not serve the world. There is nothing enlightened about shrinking so that other people won't feel insecure around you. We are all meant to shine, as children do. We were born to make manifest the glory of God that is within us. It's not just in some of us; it's in everyone. And as we let our own light shine, we unconsciously give other people permission to do the same. As we are liberated from our own fear, our presence automatically liberates others.[77]

CHAMPIONS ARE NOT AFRAID OF HARD WORK

When we wish to lose weight, we put off doing exercise because it means we have to exert ourselves. When we think of engaging in a new business venture, we hardly pursue it because it demands sacrifice, commitment, and hard work. We complain about not getting what we want, but what are we doing to *work* toward that thing? How can a farmer harvest his wheat when he did not plow his soil and sow his seeds?

What you sow is what you reap—if you sow a whole lot of nothing, you will reap a harvest of nothing. Sow little; receive little. Sow more; reap more. Sowing *and* reaping, for the most part, is labor intensive. Even while you wait for fruit to come, you must continually cultivate, protect, and nurture the crop. You must apply absolute and honest hard work. That's the only way to succeed at fulfilling your dreams.

CHAMPIONS ARE FULL OF PASSION

Successful musicians, singers, actors, painters, doctors, etc. are all passionate about their chosen careers. Their passion drives them to conquer their fears. Their strong desire to succeed in their field propels them to invest more hard work simply in order to improve their craft. Individuals who constantly fail in their endeavors are those who are not passionate about what they are doing. They don't feel the powerful urge to fulfill their goals and reach their dreams. They are not motivated because they haven't tapped into their intrinsic values and objectives.

In order for you to be fully successful, you should look inward—deep into your soul, mind, and heart—and discover what excites you, moves you to action, and makes you want to jump out of bed in the morning. What are you truly passionate about? Is it your desire to help people, coordinate events, speak out about injustice, write poetry, see the world, or create something with your hands? Find out what inspires you! Understanding what intrinsically motivates you will guide and compel you to work harder with a renewed determination and confidence.

CHAMPIONS MOTIVATE THEMSELVES

Another reason for our *mañana* habit is our lack of self-motivation. Our lack of motivation will cause us to make excuses—we will convince ourselves we must wait for someone else or something else to happen before we a can take action. Our motivation actually comes from somewhere outside of ourselves, and unless there is that external provocation or encouragement, we are not motivated to move forward. Your success does not depend on someone or something else. Nor is it healthy for you physically, mentally, emotionally, or spiritually to be passive about *your* life and *your* success. The drive to achieve must come from within you. You must be your own best fan, coach, cheerleader, and confidante. Tell yourself every morning, "If it is to be, it's up to me!"

Let me remind you that a large percentage of people around you will always be against you fulfilling your dreams. And it's not necessarily the people but the enemy working behind them who is determined to distract, derail, and destroy your best efforts. If you want to be successful, you must learn to keep yourself on target and fire up your inner motivation; you must be like a self-charging battery and never let your engine die. Find out what really drives you. Don't remain idle, but get yourself in gear and running at full throttle.

Elizabeth Kubler Ross once said, "People are like stained-glass windows. They sparkle and shine when the sun is out, but when the darkness sets in, their true beauty is revealed only if there is a light from within."[78]

CHAMPIONS KNOW HOW TO CONDITION THEIR MINDS FOR PEAK PERFORMANCE

Champions routinely use the morning to condition their mind and body for peak performance. They live by a creed. They practice establishing a certain mindset and discipline their thought patterns. They use verbal affirmations on a daily basis to condition their mind for peak performance.

According to Lisa Gates, life coach and writer,

> Declarations are timeless statements of purpose in the present tense, designed to create ongoing quality of life shifts.
>
> Declarations stem from who you are and what you value, and point to your vision. They may sound bold and completely outrageous, perhaps even a little wild—but not impossible.
>
> Practically speaking, declarations inform your goals, not the other way around. So, once you've finished your declarations, listing your top goal in each area (that's right, just one) should come easily and organically.[79]

I challenge you to implement a success creed for the next thirty days. If you speak out and live by a creed that you have embraced—spirit, soul, and body—I guarantee that after thirty days you will begin to push past limitations, barriers, and challenges (including every social, emotional, physical, and economic obstacle, to a new level of success and freedom. You will be on your way to living the life of your dreams. Below is my personal creed that I speak out over my own life every single day.

THE CREED

Because I am fearfully and wonderfully made, created in the nature and image of God as a success-oriented being, I have the courage and personal integrity to:

- Be myself
- Celebrate my strengths
- Eradicate my weaknesses
- Ask for what I need

- Desire what I want
- Dream of a better life
- Wake up and live the life of my dreams
- Enjoy today
- Believe that tomorrow will be better than today
- Voice my opinion
- Pursue my goals
- Change my mind
- Break self-destructive habits, thoughts, and cycles of failure
- Change for the best
- Be my best
- Give my best
- Do my best
- Put my best foot forward
- Enjoy giving and receiving love
- Face and transform my fear
- Seek and ask for help and support when I need it
- Spring free from the superwoman trap
- Stop being all things to everyone
- Trust myself to know what is right for me
- Make my own decision based on my perceptions of options
- Befriend myself
- Be totally honest with myself
- Respect my vulnerabilities
- Heal old and current wounds

- Acquire new, good, and useful habits—and eliminate the bad
- Complete unfinished business
- View my failures as life lessons
- Turn my losses into gain
- Realize that I have emotional and practical rights
- Honor my commitments
- Keep my promises
- Give myself credit for my accomplishments
- Love the little girl in me
- Overcome my need for approval
- Grant myself permission to laugh out loud
- Play as hard as I can
- Dance like no one is watching
- Sing at the top of my voice
- Catch butterflies
- Color outside of the lines
- Watch Mother Nature as she tucks in the sun for a good night's sleep, and then turns the night-lights on for my enjoyment, security, and pleasure
- Witness the dawning of a new day as the sun rubs the lingering sleepiness from its eyes
- To choose life over death
- To choose success over failure
- Live with an attitude of gratitude
- Quit being a trash receptacle and dumping bin
- Rid myself of toxic relationships

- Pursue and develop healthy and supportive relationships
- Renegotiate the terms of all relationships
- Nurture myself like I nurture others
- Take "me moments"
- Be alone without feeling guilty
- Demand people give to me as much as I give to them
- Manage my time
- Demand that others value my time
- Be more objective about my feelings and more subjective about my thoughts
- Detoxify all areas of my life
- Take an emotional enema when necessary
- Nurture others because I want to, not because I have to
- Choose what is right for me
- Insist on being paid fairly for what I do
- Say "no" and mean it
- Know when enough is enough
- Put an end to toxic cycles
- Set limits and boundaries
- Say "yes" only when I really mean it
- Have realistic expectations
- Take risks and accept change
- Live morally
- Conduct my affairs ethically
- Grow through change

- Grow through challenges
- Give others permission to grow and to be themselves
- To break glass ceilings
- To live beyond the limits
- To set new goals
- Savor the mystery of the Holy Spirit
- Pray and expect an exceptional and favorable outcome
- Meditate in order to unclutter my mind
- Wave good-bye to guilt, self-doubt, rejection, and insecurity
- De-weed the flowerbed of my thought life
- Treat myself with respect and teach others to do the same
- Fill my cup first and then refresh others from the overflow
- Demand excellence from myself and others
- Plan for the future but live in the present
- Value my insight, intelligence, and wisdom
- Know that I am loveable
- Celebrate the differences in others
- Make forgiveness a priority

I have the courage to:

- Accept myself just as I am, now and forever
- Live within my means
- Love God
- Manifest His divinity

- Breathe beyond innate fears by living in the realm of faith
- Embrace God's Spirit, knowing that it is stronger and wiser than mine
- Prosper beyond my imagination
- Give more than I receive
- Give to those who can never return the favor
- Love unconditionally
- Live consciously

Therefore:

- I will give God the time He needs
- I will give my mind the order it needs
- I will give my life the discipline it needs
- I will give my spirit the freedom it needs
- I will give my soul the love it needs
- I will give my body the nourishment and exercise it needs
- I will give my voice the platform it needs
- I will give myself the love and attention I need
- I will pursue my dreams and accomplish my goals
- I will give to others
- I will pursue my purpose and maximize my potential
- I will stand on truth, and take a stand for truth
- I will positively impact my generation
- I will positively influence a system and/or an institution
- I will live, learn, love, serve, and then leave a legacy

- I am on a collision course with destiny
- I am at the intersection of truth

  On the avenue of opportunity

  In the boulevard of passion

  At a street named courage

  All lights are green

- I choose to proceed
- Today I walk away with purpose, success, and nobility
- Today and always I alone accept and own full and total responsibility for being my genuine and true self and therefore vow to live authentically; to grow and care for my best and nobler self, that I may reflect the shimmer of God's glory and divinity.

This is my contract with myself, and today I give myself permission to PUSH until I succeed!

> *To him whose elastic and vigorous thought*
> *keeps pace with the sun, the day is a perpetual*
> *morning.* —HENRY DAVID THOREAU

> *In the beauties of holiness, from the womb of the morning,*
> *You have the dew of Your youth.* —PSALM 110:3

> *All the flowers of all the tomorrows are in the*
> *seeds of today.* —AUTHOR UNKNOWN

IN CONCLUSION

The apostle Paul said in Philippians 3:14, *"I press toward the mark for the prize of the high calling of God in Christ Jesus"* (KJV). He was prepared to push through until he broke into that place in God where he found pure expression of destiny and purpose. Sometimes, like the Israelites, we must take an indirect route to get there. I want to encourage you not to give up on your dreams when faced with challenges or when your trajectory ceases to become a straight path. Do not give up on your dreams because God is not through with you.

When you feel yourself slipping, just remember Sparky. He was not even disliked by his other classmates; he wasn't important enough for that. He was the invisible kid at school and was astonished if a schoolmate ever said "hello" to him outside school hours. School was all but impossible for Sparky. He failed every subject in the eighth grade. He flunked physics, algebra, and English in high school. He didn't do much better in sports. He was clumsy, uncoordinated, and untalented. Although he did manage to make the school golf team, he lost the only important match of the year. There was a consolation match and he lost that too.

Throughout his youth, Sparky was socially awkward. He never once asked a girl out. He presented himself as nondescript: simple, bland, unassuming—just another face in the crowd. With his regular looks, he passed for ordinary so easily that most people believed him when he insisted, as he did so often in later years, that he was a "nothing," a "nobody," an "uncomplicated man with ordinary interests." With the exception of his ability to draw and sketch, he was a pitiful failure at everything else. He was proud of his artwork, though, and while no one else appreciated it, Sparky had found his passion.

Upon graduating from high school, he wrote a letter to Walt Disney Studios. He was told to send some samples of his artwork. He spent a great deal of time on it, and finally submitted something. The reply from the Disney Studios came. He had been rejected once again. After a stint in the military, Sparky wrote his own autobiography in cartoons, focusing on the kid who could never accomplish anything. He described his childhood self, a little-boy loser and chronic underachiever who had a female friend who constantly rejected him. He was the little cartoon boy whose kite would never fly, who never succeeded in kicking the football, whose Christmas tree was never quite right, whose loud mouth gal pal never appreciated him nor had faith in him, and who became the most famous cartoon character of all—Charlie Brown!

Sparky, the boy who failed at everything and whose work was rejected repeatedly, was Charles Schulz. Charles Schulz persevered. He succeeded beyond his wildest imagination. He earned and deserved that success. He endured rejection. It took lots of failing and falling, but he never quit. *Peanuts* ran for nearly fifty years without interruption and appeared in more than 2,600 newspapers in seventy-five countries. Charles Schulz held on to his dream, and because he did, the world today is a richer and brighter place.[80]

I pray that you will persevere too. Do not give up on your dreams. God is up to something great and He has you in mind. You are loaded with something spectacular...

Persevere Until Something Happens—PUSH until it manifests...

Take hold of the birthing power of prayer today!

EPILOGUE

THE BUTTERFLY'S STRUGGLE

Author unknown

A man found a cocoon of a butterfly. One day a small opening appeared. He sat and watched the butterfly for several hours as it struggled to force its body through that little hole.

Then it seemed to stop making any progress. It appeared as if it had gotten as far as it could, and it could go no further. So the man decided to help the butterfly. He took a pair of scissors and snipped off the remaining bit of the cocoon.

The butterfly then emerged easily. But it had a swollen body and small, shriveled wings. The man continued to watch the butterfly because he expected that, at any moment, the wings would enlarge and expand to be able to support the body, which would contract in time.

Neither happened! In fact, the butterfly spent the rest of its life crawling around with a swollen body and shriveled wings. It never was able to fly.

What the man, in his kindness and haste, did not understand, was that the restricting cocoon and the struggle required for the butterfly to get through the tiny opening were God's way of forcing fluid from the body of the butterfly into its wings, so that it would be ready for flight once it achieved its freedom from the cocoon.

Sometimes struggles are exactly what we need in our lives. If God allowed us to go through our lives without any obstacles, it would cripple us. We would not be as strong as what we could have been. We could never fly!

I asked for strength—God gave me difficulties to make me strong.

I asked for wisdom—God gave me problems to solve.

I asked for prosperity—God gave me a brain and brawn to work.

I asked for courage—God gave me danger to overcome.

I asked for love—God gave me troubled people to help.

I asked for favors—God gave me opportunities.

I received nothing I wanted—but I received everything I needed!

May your path be bright and full of light everywhere you go.

I pray your feet will never stumble out of God's plan.

May the desires of your heart come true, and may you experience peace in everything you do.

May goodness, kindness, and mercy come your way, and may you gain wisdom and grow in the Lord every day.

ENDNOTES

1. Matthew Henry, *Commentary on the Whole Bible* (Grand Rapids: Zondervan Pub. House, 1961), http://www.biblestudytools.com/commentaries/matthew-henry-concise/revelation/12.html.

2. Kim Wildner, *Mother's Intention: How Belief Shapes Birth* (Ludington, MI: Harbor & Hill, 2003), 74.

3. "Concipio," Latin Word List, accessed December 10, 2013, http://www.latinwordlist.com/latin-words/concipio-4622035.htm.

4. Faisal Malick, *The Political Spirit* (Shippensburg, PA: Destiny Image Publishers, 2008), 180.

5. John Crowder, *Miracle Workers, Reformers, and the New Mystics: How to Become Part of the Supernatural Generation* (Shippensburg, Pennsylvania: Destiny Image Publishers, Inc., 2006), 275.

6. Encarta® World English Dictionary © 1999 Microsoft Corporation. All rights reserved.

7. Malick, Political Spirit, 175.

8. W. E. Vine, *Vine's Expository Dictionary of Old and New Testament Words* (Old Tappan, NJ: F.H. Revell, 1981), http://www2.mf.no/bibelprog/vines.pl?word=womb.

9. Dutch Sheets, *Intercessory Prayer* (Ventura, California: Regal Books, 1996), 116.

10. Ibid. 127.

11. Barbara Katz Rothman, "About This Site," Barbara Katz Rothman, 2011, http://www.barbarakatzrothman.com/.

12. *The American Heritage Dictionary of the English Language.*, 4th ed. (Boston: Houghton Mifflin, 2000), s.v. "midwife," http://www.thefreedictionary.com/midwife.

13. Sarah Zadok, "Midwives: Pioneers of Faith," The Jewish Woman, accessed December 11, 2013, http://www.chabad.org/theJewishWoman/article_cdo/aid/461823/jewish/Midwives.htm.

14. Peter M. Dunn, "Perinatal Lessons from the Past," Arch Dis Child Fetal Neonatal, 1998, 78, http://europepmc.org/articles/PMC1720814/pdf/v079p00F77.pdf.

15. Ibid.

16. Zadok, "Midwives: Pioneers of Faith."

17. Ibid.

18. "In Focus: Jewish Midwives," Jewish Women's Archive, accessed December 11, 2013, http://jwa.org/discover/infocus/midwives.

19. "Torah on the Web," The Israel Koschitzky Virtual Beit Midrash, 1996, http://www.vbm-torah.org/archive/intparsha/shemot/13-57shmot.doc.

20. "Yocheved," Hebrewletters.com, accessed December 11, 2013, http://www.hebrewletters.com/item.cfm?itemid=44284.

21. Leah Kohn, "Women in Judaism," Torah.org, 2000, Shifrah and Puah, Miriam and Jochebed, http://www.torah.org/learning/women/class45.html.

22. Ibid.

23. "Yocheved," Hebrewletters.com.

24. Zadok, "Midwives: Pioneers of Faith."

25. Ibid.

26. Peg Plumbo, "Pushing During Labor: Childbirth Information," iVillage, June 16, 2006, http://www.ivillage.com/pushing-during-labor-childbirth-information-ivillagecom/6-a-144608.

27. Jennifer Vanderlaan, "Physiologic Labor: Pushing," Birthing Naturally, 2013, http://www.birthingnaturally.net/birth/physiologic/pushing.html.

28. Jennifer Vanderlaan, "Labor Pain: Fear of Labor," Birthing Naturally, 2013, http://www.birthingnaturally.net/birth/pain/fear.html.

29. Christine Cadena, "Spontaneous Birthing, Pushing: Natural Labor and Delivery," Yahoo Contributor Network, December 12, 2007, http://voices.yahoo.com/spontaneous-birthing-pushing-natural-labor-delivery-693552.html.

30. "Birth Quotes," Intrinsic Birthing, accessed December 11, 2013, http://www.intrinsicbirthing.com/birth-quotes.html.

31. "A Glossary of Basic Jewish Terms and Concepts," Judaism 101, Mikvah, accessed December 11, 2013, http://www.ou.org/about/judaism/m.htm.

32. Erik Peacock, *Finding Home* (Bloomington, IN: AuthorHouse, 2012), 136.

33. Ibid.

34. "P.U.S.H. = Pray Until Something Happens!" Marriage Missions International, accessed December 11, 2013, http://www.marriagemissions.com/push.

35. Robert Southwell and William B. Turnbull, The Poetical Works of the Rev. Robert Southwell, (London: J. R. Smith, 1856), 123-124.

36. Thayer's Greek-English Lexicon, http://www.britannica.com/EBchecked/topic/177746/Ecclesia.

37. Carmella B'Hahn, "Be the Change You Wish to See: An Interview with Arun Gandhi," Reclaiming Children and Youth (Bloomington) Vol. 10, No. 1 (Spring 2001) p. 6.

38. Queen Elizabeth II, "Christmas Broadcast 1954," The Official Website of the British Monarchy, 2009, http://www.royal.gov .uk/ImagesandBroadcasts/TheQueensChristmasBroadcasts/ ChristmasBroadcasts/ChristmasBroadcast1954.aspx.

39. "Abraham married a second time; his new wife was named Keturah. She gave birth to Zimran, Jokshan, Medan, Midian, Ishbak, and Shuah. Jokshan had Sheba and Dedan. Dedan's descendants were the Asshurim, the Letushim, and the Leummim. Midian had Ephah, Epher, Hanoch, Abida, and Eldaah—all from the line of Keturah" (Genesis 25:1-4 MSG). We read in Genesis 25:6, "And while he was still living he sent them away from his son Isaac, eastward to the east country" (ESV). Abraham sent them eastward to Assyria and Persia.

40. "Meaning of the Number 9 in the Bible," Meaning of Numbers in the Bible, accessed December 12, 2013, http://www.biblestudy.org/ bibleref/meaning-of-numbers-in-bible/9.html.

41. Todd Dennis and Richard Anthony, "The Significance of the Number 40," Ecclesia.org, accessed December 11, 2013, http://www .ecclesia.org/truth/40.html.

42. "Meaning of the Number 40 in the Bible," Meaning of Numbers in the Bible, accessed December 12, 2013, http://www.biblestudy.org/ bibleref/meaning-of-numbers-in-bible/40.html.

43. Mary Antin and Werner Sollors, *The Promised Land* (New York, NY: Penguin Books, 1997), 72.

44. William Tiller, "The Faculty," Great Mystery, accessed December 11, 2013, http://www.greatmystery.org/Faculty/WilliamTiller.html.

45. William A. Tiller, "How the Power of Intention Alters Matter," Spirit of Ma'at, The Effect of Repeated Experiments, accessed December 12, 2013, http://www.spiritofmaat.com/archive/mar2/ prns/tiller.htm.

46. Ibid.

47. Ibid., The Vacuum Contains Non-Physical "Stuff."

48. Ibid., How Much Power Are We Talking About.

49. Ibid.

50. Ibid.

51. Ibid.

52. Paul Klee, Paul Klee (Bern: Benteli, 1949), 188.

53. According to the Microsoft Encarta Multimedia Encyclopedia, Copyright © 2009.

54. Originally from http://en.wikipedia.org/wiki/Thought.

55. Elliott Jaques, *The Life and Behavior of Living Organisms* (Westport, CT: Praeger, 2002), 237.

56. Darcy Andries, *The Secret of Success is Not a Secret* (South Portland, Maine: Sellers Publishing Inc., 2008), 292.

57. Kris Cole, *Complete Idiot's Guide to Clear Communication* (Indianapolis, IN: Alpha, 2002), 59.

58. Daniel Todd Gilbert, *Stumbling on Happiness* (New York, NY: A.A. Knopf, 2006), 5.

59. Nikola Tesla, *My Inventions: The Autobiography of Nikola Tesla* (Williston, VT: Hart Bros., 1982), 13.

60. Ibid., 49.

61. Taken from the "The Carpenter," Author Unknown.

62. "Thought Provokers," Ecclesia.org, Rich and Poor, accessed December 12, 2013, http://www.ecclesia.org/truth/thought.html.

63. Theodore Roosevelt, "Citizenship in a Republic" (speech, Sorbonne, Paris, France, April 23, 1910), http://www.theodore-roosevelt.com/images/research/speeches/maninthearena.pdf.

64. J.K. Rowling and Mary GrandPré, *Harry Potter and the Chamber of Secrets* (New York, NY: Arthur A. Levine Books, 1999), 333.

65. "Genius," accessed December 12, 2013, http://en.wiktionary.org/wiki/genius.

66. Steven Pressfield, *The War of Art: Break Through the Blocks and Win You Inner Creative Battles* (New York, NY: Grand Central Publishing, 2002).

67. Marianne Williamson, *A Return to Love* (New York, NY: HarperCollins, 1992), 191.

68. Michael Miles, "Taking Responsibility: There Is Always a Choice," Dumb Little Man: Tips for Life, September 13, 2008, Every Moment Is a New Choice, http://www.dumblittleman.com/2008/09/taking-responsibility-there-is-always.html.

69. H. Jackson Brown, *P.S. I Love You* (Nashville, TN: Thomas Nelson, 1991), 13.

70. Kenneth Hildebrand, *Achieving Real Happiness* (New York, NY: Harper, 1955).

71 Unknown Author, qtd. in Brennan Manning, *Ruthless Trust: The Ragamuffin's Path to God* (San Francisco, CA: HarperCollins, 2002), 133-135.

72. Lou Ferrigno, "When Life Gives You Lemons," Lou Ferrigno Official Site, accessed December 12, 2013, http://louferrigno.com/if-life-gives-you-lemons.

73. Andries, *The Secret of Success is Not a Secret.*

74. "Americans Watching More TV Than Ever," Newswire, May 20, 2009, http://www.nielsen.com/us/en/newswire/2009/americans-watching-more-tv-than-ever.html.

75. "Thanks for Your Time," Motivateus.com, October 3, 2008, http://www.motivateus.com/stories/have-you-learned-this-yet.htm.

76. Author Unknown, text reproduced in full at http://www.rogerknapp.com/inspire/yesterdaytomorrow.htm.

77. Williamson, *A Return to Love*, 191.

78. Elisabeth Kübler-Ross, qtd. in Jim Clemmer, The Leader's Digest: Timeless Principles for Team and Organization Success (Kitchener, Ontario: TCG Press, 2003), 84.

79. Lisa Gates, "Goal Setting from the Inside Out," Personal Development for Personal Success Forums, March 2009, http://www.shamoublog.com/forum/archive/index.php?t-900.html.

80. Andries, *The Secret of Success is Not a Secret,* http://www.topachievement.com/persevere.html.

OTHER BOOKS BY DR. N. CINDY TRIMM

The Commanding Your Morning Daily Devotional

'Til Heaven Invades Earth

When Kingdoms Clash

The Prayer Warrior's Way

The Art of War for Spiritual Battle

Commanding Your Morning

The Rules of Engagement

Join the

Soul Fast
MOVEMENT

—————— *with* ——————

DR. CINDY TRIMM

Find out more about Dr. Trimm's new
courses and resources for your family, women's
group or church and SAVE even more!

Join today at:
www.SoulFastMovement.com